The
CROSS-STITCH
GARDEN

First published in Great Britain 2016

Search Press Limited
Wellwood, North Farm Road,
Tunbridge Wells, Kent TN2 3DR

Aoki Kazuko no Cross Stitch Wild Flower Garden by Kazuko Aoki
Copyright © 2002 Kazuko Aoki

Publisher: Sunao Onuma
Photographer: Yasuo Nagumo
Original Book Design: Kayoko Wakayama (L'espace)
Tracing: Satomi D. (day studio)
Instruction Diagrams: Noriko Yamamura
Project Assistance: Noriko Ishimura, Etsuko Endo, Fukiko Enya, Sanae Okuda, Setsuko
Konno, Kazuko Sanjo, Yukiko Shibata, Keiko Hasui, Akemi Honjo, and Michiko Yoshii
Translator: Kyoko Matthews
Book Design: Arati Devasher, www.aratidevasher.com

English edition published by arrangement with EDUCATIONAL FOUNDATION BUNKA
GAKUEN BUNKA PUGLISHING BUREAU through the English Agency (Japan) Ltd.
English-language translation and production by World Book Media, LLC.
Email: info@worldbookmedia.com

ISBN: 978-1-78221-331-4

The Publishers and author can accept no responsibility for any consequences arising
from the information, advice or instructions given in this publication.

Readers are permitted to reproduce any of the items in this book for their personal
use, or for the purposes of selling for charity, free of charge and without the prior
permission of the Publishers. Any use of the items for commercial purposes is not
permitted without the prior permission of the Publishers.

Suppliers
If you have difficulty in obtaining any of the materials and equipment mentioned in
this book, then please visit the Search Press website for details of suppliers:
www.searchpress.com

Printed in China

10 9 8 7 6 5 4 3 2 1

The CROSS-STITCH GARDEN

Over 70 cross-stitch motifs with 20 stunning projects

Kazuko Aoki

SEARCH PRESS

Introduction

I started gardening with one aim in mind: to grow a few flowers for my table. Little did I imagine that gardening would become part of my daily life, not to mention one of my favourite hobbies.

Upon planting my first garden, I became transfixed by the way sunlight would stream through the leaves and pink roses and blue flowers would blow in the breeze just outside my studio door. The beauty of my garden was so distracting that I became unable to concentrate on my embroidery!

As a result, I decided to combine my love of gardening with my embroidery so that I could enjoy both passions at the same time. I love to embroider the flowers that grow in my garden so that I can run outside and study the shape of a stamen or the colour of a petal. Sometimes, I plant seeds for a certain type of flower that I want to embroider, then wait in anticipation as they bloom.

This book is dedicated to those who love both gardening and needlework. I hope to share the beauty and color of my small garden, as well as the sense of wonder and curiosity that it inspires in my heart.

— Kazuko Aoki

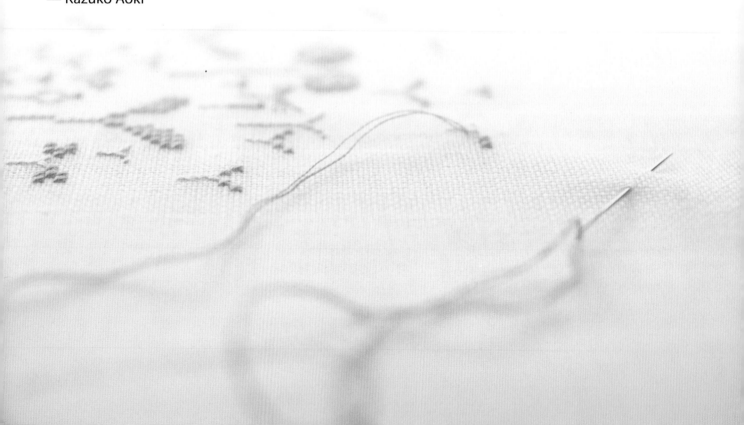

Contents

Red campion

wild mignonette

Pansy Motifs

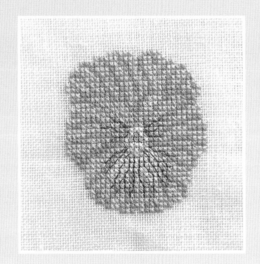

Romeo & Juliet

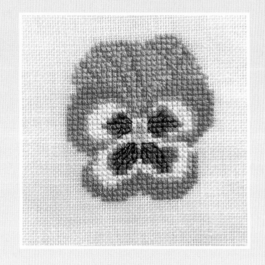

Rosalin

Prelude Scarlet

Crystal Rose

I plant multiple varieties of pansies each year. I love the Romeo and Juliet for its soft and subtle shades of apricot and salmon, while the Shalon boasts a more vibrant colour combination and fringed appearance. Pansies exhibit such a great variety of hue and saturation that I could sketch them for hours.

Instructions on page 56

Iona Blue

Crystal Deep Blue

Marina

Shalon

Pansy Coin Purse

A single pansy embellishes this dainty coin purse. Use this sweet little pouch to store change or your favourite lipstick.

Instructions on page 58

To design your own pansy motifs, sketch the flower on a sheet of graph paper, then shade in each box with your desired colour scheme.

It is especially important to keep the wrong side of your work tidy when using bright floss to embroider a light background fabric.

Viola Sampler & Motifs

Over the past few years, many advancements have been made in breeding violas and there are now more varieties than ever before. Each year, I look forward to choosing my favourites from my seed catalogue. I especially love the varieties with names that sound more like desserts than flowers, including Sherbet Lemon Chiffon and Blueberry Cream. Violas are so enjoyable to embroider because they exhibit such as broad range of colour. To find the perfect shades, I hold the embroidery floss next to the flower and select the closest match. Stitch up a few of the viola motifs on pages 11–13 or the viola sampler shown above, or have fun designing your own colour schemes for this versatile flower.

Instructions on pages 61 & 62

Sherbet Lemon Chiffon

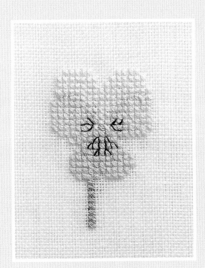

Penny Orange

Fancy Mix

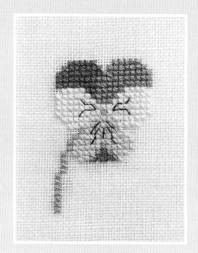

Heartsease

Violet Stela

Bambini

Fancy Mix 2

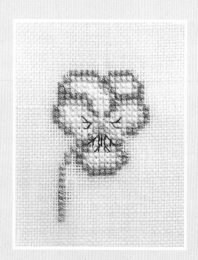

Blue Swirl

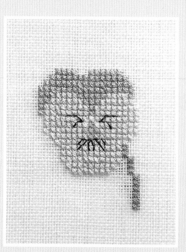

Sherbet Lilac Ice

Blue Face

Blueberry Cream

Baby Light Blue

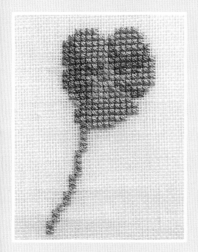

Baby Light Blue

Velour Blue Bronze

Black Jack

Common Wildflowers

I admire wildflowers for their strength and resilience. Whether it's by the side of the road or in a vacant lot, it is always so refreshing to see wildflowers growing in the most unlikely places. Some of my favourites include common vetch, Indian strawberry and shepherd's purse. I've designed individual motifs for these flowers, plus a wreath sampler featuring a beautiful assortment of wildflowers.

Instructions on page 65

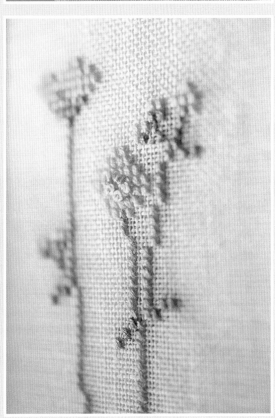

Red Poppy Collage

I always try to include a splash of red when designing a garden because it adds an element of depth. I usually rely on geraniums to provide that rich red shade; however, I was tempted to plant some poppy seeds one year. I'm not sure if it was the bad weather we had that season or excessive fertilisation on my part, but sadly, my poppies died almost as soon as they bloomed. Luckily, I had just enough time to immortalise them in my sketchbook. I was inspired to create this poppy collage featuring a patchwork background and appliquéd ribbon.

Instructions on page 68

Wildflower Garden Sampler & Motifs

My interest in wildflowers first arose when I planted a packet of mixed wildflower seeds from Suttons Seeds. Before long, sprouts of all shapes and sizes began popping up. I loved guessing which flowers would bloom from these cute little seedlings and would use *Reader's Digest Field Guide to the Wild Flowers of Britain* to identify the plants.

Instructions on pages 70 & 73

I was inspired to plant wild mignonette after reading *The Secret Garden*. Wild mignonette is so unassuming that you might mistake it for a weed; however, it possesses a special ability to highlight the beauty of other flowers in the garden.

Also known as viola tricolor and heartsease, this plant is native to northern Europe. While visiting Sweden, I noticed an abundance of these flowers blooming in the woods and wondered who had planted them. Upon further research, I discovered that this flower is actually the wild ancestor of cultivated pansies.

As one of the most common wildflowers in the world, you've probably seen white clovers growing in fields. Interestingly, white clover is not native to Japan, but arrived on ships from the Netherlands during the 1800s.

Also called hardy geranium, this plant is known for its large violet blue flowers. I planted a few seeds in my garden and although they bloomed at first, these flowers later became scarce.

Actually a member of the bean family, the everlasting pea is an extremely fast growing plant with climbing vines and beautiful flowers.

Red campion

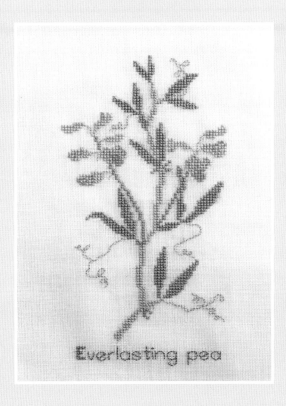

Everlasting pea

While vacationing in England, I often admired red campion blooming in the wilderness. Recently, this flower has become readily available in potted plant form throughout Japan.

Wild Rose Sampler

Over the years, I have collected nearly 90 different types of roses.
While I love the deep scent and elegant beauty of English roses, wild
roses will always occupy a special place in my heart.

Instructions on page 76

Wild Rose Journal

With its apple-scented leaves and multitude of bright red rose hips, the Rosa eglanteria is one of my favourite wild roses. I designed this book-shaped sampler in honour of this characteristically wild rose. I recommend displaying this sampler in a deep shadow box frame.

Instructions on page 78

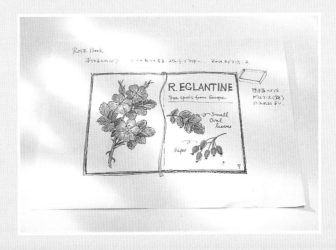

25

Berry Motifs

The first time I visited the English countryside, I was impressed by a magnificent blackberry hedge. I was amazed by the beautiful pink flowers and shiny black berries growing among the tangled branches. Upon returning home, I started growing a few different kinds of berry plants in pots, but they produced very little fruit. Now, I grow berries in my garden and am filled with wonder every time the flowers transform into fruit.

Instructions on page 80

Berry Tote Bag

Beads are the perfect medium for depicting the texture of berries. There's no need to count the beads, just align them until they fill the outline of the berry. I designed this tote bag to showcase the beautiful fruit and foliage of my beloved berry plants. This design makes a great summer purse or can be used to transport produce from the farmers' market.

Instructions on page 82

Christmas Rose

After all my other plants have gone to sleep for the winter, the Christmas rose blooms in solitude. The Helleborus niger, which is a white Christmas rose, blooms at the end of January. My garden also includes the gorgeous Orientalis, which features a gradation of colours ranging from white to pink to dark wine. Many of these flowers have little patches of colour which I like to think of as freckles!

Instructions on page 84

H. niger

Yellow Flowers

For a short period of time each spring, borders of yellow flowers
appear along the pathways near my house. Seeing these cheerful,
sunny flowers always brightens my mood.

Instructions on page 86

Blue Flowers

Blue flowers exhibit such a broad range of colour—from the light blue of clover to the deep periwinkle blue of anemone. Look closely at the center of the anemone and you will see a black core.

Instructions on page 86

Swedish Wildflowers
Collage & Sampler

I attended textile school in Boras, Sweden, which is about a four hour train ride from Stockholm. Although I was very busy learning how to weave fabric, I often enjoyed walking through the picturesque woods of northern Europe. I learned that Sweden has a long winter and a very short spring and summer. Wood anemones bloom when there was no sign of them a week ago and the pasture grass sprouts up so quickly you can practically watch it grow. A friend of mine taught me how to make wreaths from flowers, so I would decorate my room with the flowers I collected on my walks. This was the start of my love affair with wildflowers.

Instructions on pages 88 & 92

Wildlife Garden Collage

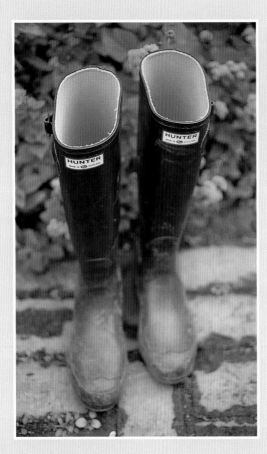 

This collage was inspired by wildlife gardens, which are designed to attract friendly insects and animals. Certain creatures, such as ladybugs, bees and frogs can help a garden flourish by pollinating the flowers and eating destructive insects. To encourage their presence in your garden, try planting some of their favourite flowers, including the white lace flower, yarrow, nemophila, convolvulus arvensis and iberis. In my opinion, a garden is never more beautiful than when it's full of life.

Instructions on page 94

Gardening Pin Cushions & Sampler

This sampler features a variety of sweet little gardening-themed designs that I've created over the years. Stitch the entire sampler, or use the motifs individually. I've also included two small-scale motifs that make excellent pin cushions or lids for jars and tea cannisters. Add a few charms to bring the design to life.

Instructions on pages 96 & 98

Greenery Pillows

I believe that greenery can be just as beautiful as flowers. I've embroidered some applemint, yam and daisy leaves onto natural linen to create these simple, yet striking pillows.

Instructions on page 100

Leaf Coasters

Miniscule leaves decorate the corners of these cute coasters.
Embellish the edges with beads for a special touch.

Instructions on page 103

Bee Apron

Embellish a plain linen apron with this cheerful design. This motif was inspired by one of a garden's most important visitors: the bee. As pollinators, bees play such an important role in a healthy and productive garden. You can attract bees to your garden by planting their favorite flowers, which include geraniums, poppies, black-eyed Susans and clover.

Instructions on page 104

Embellished Dish Towels

In contrast to cotton, which grows in warm climates, linen is produced in cooler countries, often in northern Europe. Today, it is easier than ever before to buy high quality kitchen linens from the Baltic region. As I embroidered these towels, I couldn't help but imagine fields of beautiful blue flax flowers in bloom.

Instructions on page 105

If you're having a difficult time counting the woven threads of your fabric while stitching, try using waste canvas. Simply baste the waste canvas to your fabric, then cross-stitch through both layers. Once the embroidery is complete, remove the strands of waste canvas to reveal a perfectly stitched motif.

Seedlings Motif

Although seedlings don't receive as much attention as mature flowers in bloom, I find them to be worth celebrating. After all, these delicate little sprouts are the first stage in the life cycle of a flower.

Instructions on page 106

Spring Bulbs

Whenever I plant bulbs, I'm continuously amazed by the fact that they regularly bloom in a specific order: first it's the snowdrops, next come the crocuses, and finally, it's the daffodils and tulips. It's almost as if a microscopic alarm clock is hidden inside each bulb alongside the beautiful flowers and leaves that eventually emerge.

Instructions on page 107

Project Instructions

Tools & Materials

Fabric

Many cross-stitch designs call for a fabric known as Aida or Java canvas, but I recommend using an even weave linen fabric. Even weave fabrics have the same horizontal and vertical thread count, hence the name.

Even weave linen fabrics are classified by the number of threads used to weave a 1cm (⅜in) section. Most of the projects in this book use 11-count linen, which is available in natural, white and a wide variety of colours. When using 11-count linen, I often use two strands of No. 25 embroidery floss. When stitching on 11-count linen, each stitch is formed over two threads of the fabric.

Needles

I recommend using cross-stitch needles, which do not have sharp tips, for stitching the designs in this book. A No. 24 needle is suitable when cross-stitching on 11-count linen and a No. 26 needle is useful for backstitching once the cross-stitching is complete.

Experiment with different needles to determine the best size for your stitching needs. You will know you're using the correct size needle if it travels through the fabric without too much friction and without falling through. Make sure that your needle is not too thick, as this will stretch out the fabric grain and negatively influence the finished appearance of your work. The relationship between the fabric and the needle is key to a comfortable embroidery experience, so always take the time to determine the best needle for your individual project.

Thread

DMC No. 25 embroidery floss was used for all projects in this book. Always use two strands of floss, unless otherwise noted. I recommend using short lengths of floss, about 45-60cm (17¾-23¾in) long, to prevent tangles.

Techniques

All of the designs in this book are made using cross-stitch. Some of the designs use other embroidery stitches, including backstitch, straight stitch and French knots. Stitch diagrams are provided for each motif. These diagrams use symbols to indicate floss colour. Labels indicate when to use a stitch other than cross-stitch.

When starting large projects, fold your fabric into fourths and mark the exact centre. Each stitch diagram includes arrows indicating the horizontal and vertical centres of the design. Connect the pathways of these arrows to find the centre of the design on the diagram. Start stitching the centre of the design at the centre of the fabric. For small designs, you can start stitching from any point.

To start stitching, thread a needle and make a knot at the end of the floss. Insert the needle into the fabric from the right side to the wrong side. Insert the needle through to the right side of the fabric about 2.5cm (1in) away from the knot. Begin cross-stitching, working toward the knot. Once you've stitched over the 2.5cm (1in) thread tail enough to anchor it, you can cut off the knot. This technique is known as an away waste knot start. To finish a thread, bring the floss under the back of a few stitches on the wrong side of the work.

Once the embroidery is complete, pin the fabric to a board. Spray the work until damp, then stretch the fabric into shape. Let the fabric dry completely.

Stitch Guide

Cross-Stitch

A. Horizontal

Bring the thread diagonally from the bottom left to the top right, stitching over two threads of the fabric. Repeat for the necessary number of stitches, working from left to right. Cross each stitch, working from right to left, as shown below:

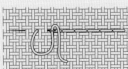

B. Vertical

With this method, you'll complete each cross-stitch individually. Make sure to always cross the thread in the same direction.

Note: Both methods A and B will create parallel stitches on the wrong side of the work.

Backstitch

Work from right to left, bringing the thread back one stitch length, then drawing it out one stitch length ahead. This stitch is often used for letters, outlines and roots.

Straight Stitch

The simplest of stitches, the straight stitch is composed of a single stitch. You can change the stitch length as desired.

French Knot

Draw the thread out at 1. Wrap the thread around the needle 2-3 times, then insert the needle back into the fabric at 2. Pull the thread in the direction of the arrow to tighten up the knot and draw the needle out on the wrong side of the work.

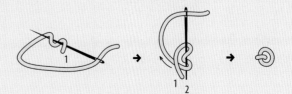

Pansy Motifs

Shown on pages 6–7

Materials (for one motif):
- » 15 x 15cm (6 x 6in) of DMC 11-count linen in 3865
- » No. 25 embroidery floss (refer to charts for DMC colour numbers)

Finished Size:
- » About 5-5.5 x 5-9cm (2-2¼ x 2-3½in)

Crystal Rose

××		3687
♡♡		3350
▲▲		3685
◆◆		725
××		907
⊠⊠		BLANC
		939

Marina

◿◿		208
◎◎		209
♥♥		333
◆◆		725
××		907
⊠⊠		BLANC
		939

Shalon

‖‖		550
◢◢		552
♠♠		208
○○		726
◆◆		725
××		907
⊠⊠		BLANC
		939

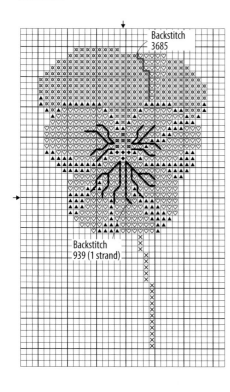

Backstitch 3685

Backstitch 939 (1 strand)

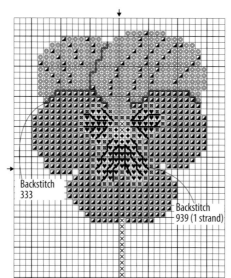

Backstitch 333

Backstitch 939 (1 strand)

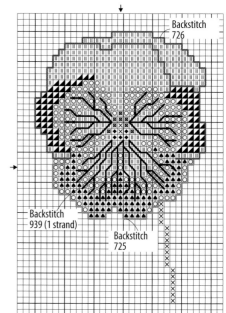

Backstitch 726

Backstitch 939 (1 strand)

Backstitch 725

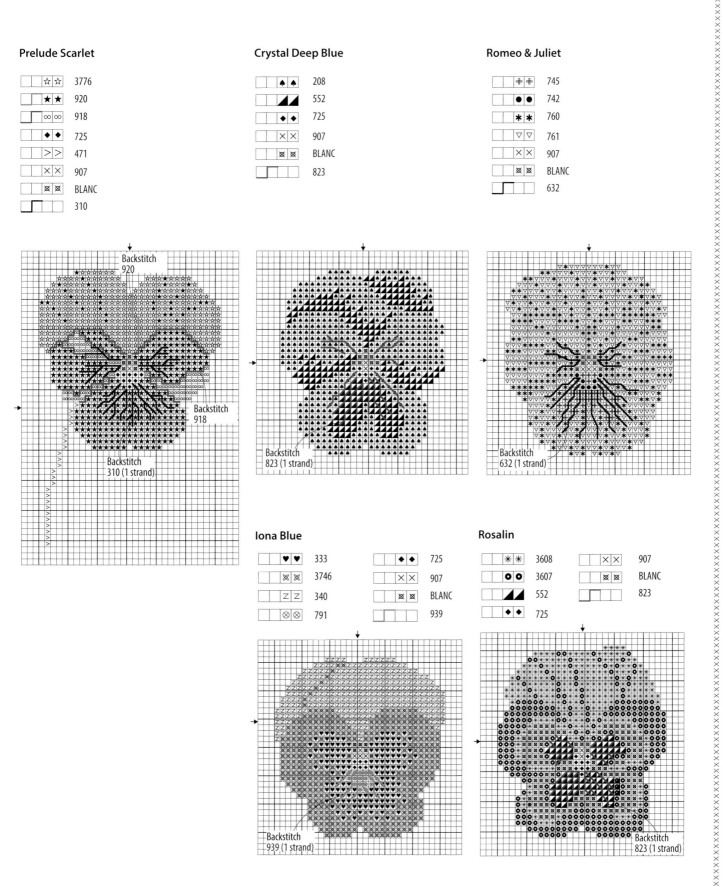

Prelude Scarlet

☆ ☆	3776
★ ★	920
∞ ∞	918
◆ ◆	725
> >	471
× ×	907
⊠ ⊠	BLANC
	310

Crystal Deep Blue

♠ ♠	208
◢◢	552
◆ ◆	725
× ×	907
⊠ ⊠	BLANC
	823

Romeo & Juliet

⊕ ⊕	745
● ●	742
✳ ✳	760
▽ ▽	761
× ×	907
⊠ ⊠	BLANC
	632

Backstitch 920

Backstitch 918

Backstitch 310 (1 strand)

Backstitch 823 (1 strand)

Backstitch 632 (1 strand)

Iona Blue

♥ ♥	333		◆ ◆	725
⊠ ⊠	3746		× ×	907
Z Z	340		⊠ ⊠	BLANC
⊗ ⊗	791			939

Rosalin

✳ ✳	3608		× ×	907
○ ○	3607		⊠ ⊠	BLANC
◢◢	552			823
◆ ◆	725

Backstitch 939 (1 strand)

Backstitch 823 (1 strand)

Pansy Coin Purse

Shown on page 8

Materials (for one purse):

» 20 x 40cm (8 x 15¾in) of DMC 11-count linen in 842
» 20 x 40cm (8 x 15¾in) of cotton fabric for lining
» No. 25 embroidery floss (refer to charts for DMC colour numbers)
» One 3.5 x 7cm (1½ x 2¾in) metal purse clasp with paper string

Tools

» Glue
» Stiletto or flat-head screwdriver
» Pliers

Finished Size:

» Embroidery: 6 x 7cm (2½ x 2¾in) for Iona Blue motif and 5.5 x 7cm (2½ x 2¾in) for Crystal Rose motif
» Coin purse: 10.5 x 13.5cm (4¼ x 5¼in)

Iona Blue

♥ ♥	333
⊠ ⊠	3746
z z	340
⊗ ⊗	791
◆ ◆	725
✕ ✕	907
⊠ ⊠	BLANC
	939

Crystal Rose

◖ ◖	3350
▲ ▲	3685
⋈ ⋈	3687
◆ ◆	725
✕ ✕	907
⊠ ⊠	BLANC
	939

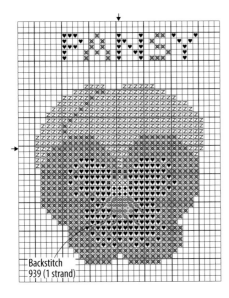

Backstitch
939 (1 strand)

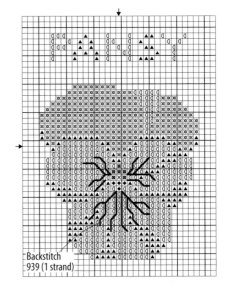

Backstitch
939 (1 strand)

Instructions

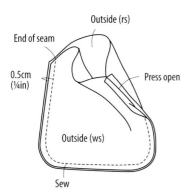

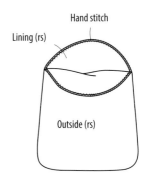

1. Cut two purse outsides and two purse linings using the template on page 60. Stitch the desired pansy motif onto one purse outside, making sure to center the motif. Align the two purse outsides with right sides together and sew along the sides and bottom using 0.5cm (¼in) seam allowance. Follow the same process to sew the two purse linings together. Press the seam allowances open.

2. With right sides facing out, insert the lining into the purse outside. Hand stitch the lining and purse outside together along the opening.

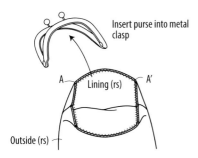

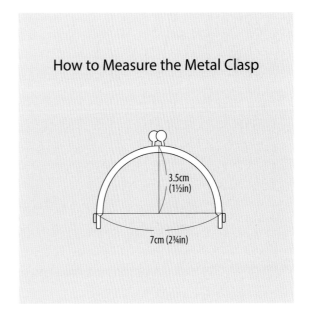

How to Measure the Metal Clasp

3. Apply glue to the inside groove on one half of the metal purse clasp. Insert the purse into the groove between points A and A'.

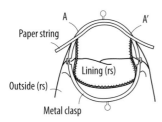

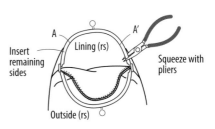

4. Cut a length of paper string equal to one half of the metal purse clasp. Use a stiletto or flat-head screwdriver to push the paper string into the metal clasp between points A and A'.

5. Insert the two remaining sides of the purse opening and the paper string into the metal clasp. Use a pair of pliers to squeeze the metal clasp closed above each hinge. Note: Use a scrap of fabric to prevent scratching the metal clasp. Let the glue dry, then repeat steps 3-5 for the other half of the purse.

6. The coin purse is complete.

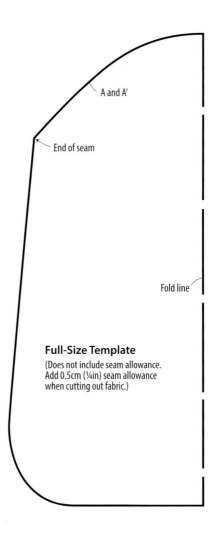

A and A'

End of seam

Fold line

Full-Size Template
(Does not include seam allowance. Add 0.5cm (¼in) seam allowance when cutting out fabric.)

Viola Sampler

Shown on page 10

Materials:

» 30 x 30cm (11¾ x 11¾in) of DMC 11-count linen in 3865
» No. 25 embroidery floss (refer to chart for DMC colour numbers)
» One 16 x 17.5cm (6¼ x 7in) collage-style wooden frame

Finished Size:

» Embroidery: 12 x 13.5cm (4¾ x 5¼in)
» Frame: 16 x 17.5cm (6¼ x 7in)

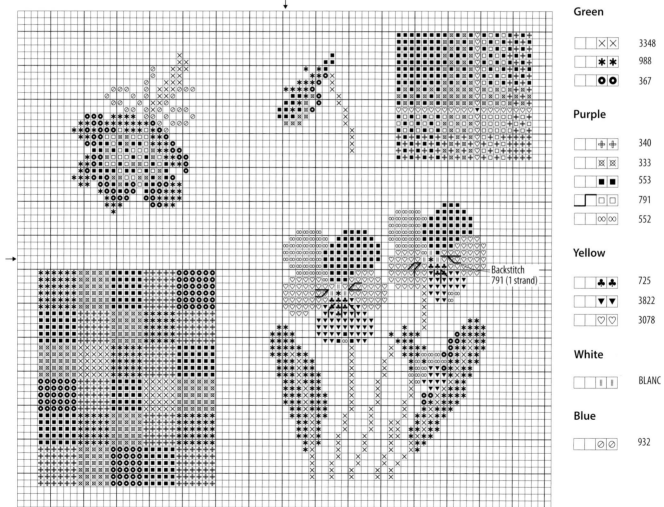

Backstitch
791 (1 strand)

Green

		3348
×	×	
✱	✱	988
●	●	367

Purple

⊕	⊕	340
⊠	⊠	333
■	■	553
□	□	791
∞	∞	552

Yellow

♣	♣	725
▼	▼	3822
♡	♡	3078

White

| ‖ | ‖ | BLANC |

Blue

| ⊘ | ⊘ | 932 |

Note: This sampler was designed to fit in a collage-style frame with different size windows. For this type of frame, use pencil to mark the position of each window on your embroidery fabric prior to stitching. Don't worry if your stitching does not align with the window of the frame; simply cut out the embroidery and mount it on another piece of fabric that is correctly aligned with the frame.

Viola Motifs

Shown on pages 11–13

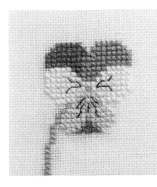

Materials (for one motif):
» 15 x 15cm (6 x 6in) of DMC 11-count linen in 3865
» No. 25 embroidery floss (refer to charts for DMC colour numbers)

Finished Size:
» About 3-3.5 x 4-6cm (1¼-1½ x 1½-2½in)

Sherbet Lemon Chiffon

◆ ◆		977
‖ ‖		3820
□ □		726
✕ ✕		471
∞ ∞		BLANC
		976
		938

Baby Light Blue

☆ ☆		340
✳ ✳		3746
◆ ◆		792
● ●		725
✕ ✕		471
⊠ ⊠		BLANC
		823

Fancy Mix 2

Z Z		3687
▼ ▼		3803
♣ ♣		3830
○ ○		725
✕ ✕		471
∞ ∞		BLANC
		938

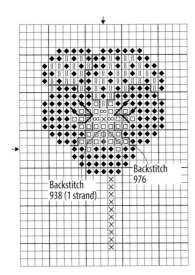

Backstitch 976

Backstitch 938 (1 strand)

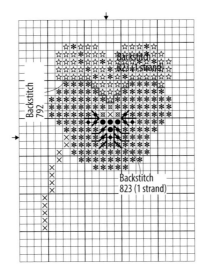

Backstitch 792

Backstitch 823 (1 strand)

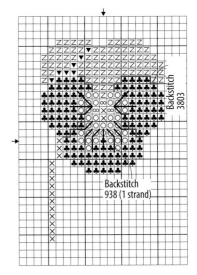

Backstitch 3803

Backstitch 938 (1 strand)

Heartsease

		552
	♠♠	552
	◇◇	3078
	●●	725
	◎◎	3822
	♥♥	553
	✕✕	471
	⊠⊠	BLANC
		791

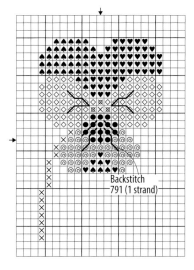

Backstitch
791 (1 strand)

Sherbert Lilac Ice

	▲▲	210
	ZZ	211
	==	972
	✕✕	471
	⊠⊠	BLANC
		823

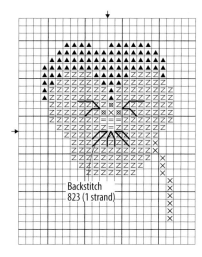

Backstitch
823 (1 strand)

Violet Stela

	◤◤	550
	♡♡	209
	♠♠	552
	ZZ	221
	==	972
	◎◎	726
	✕✕	471
	⊠⊠	BLANC
		939

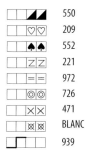

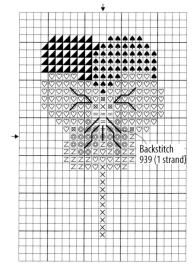

Backstitch
939 (1 strand)

Bambini

	⊠⊠	327
	⊥⊥	3803
	●●	725
	◉◉	938
	◤◤	3721
	✕✕	471
	⊠⊠	BLANC

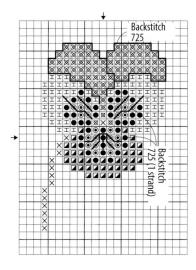

Backstitch
725

Backstitch
725 (1 strand)

Blue Swirl

	★★	209
	◇◇	211
	○○	725
	✕✕	471
	∞∞	BLANC
		550

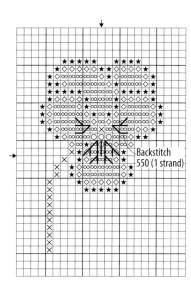

Backstitch
550 (1 strand)

Penny Orange

	▽▽	445
	◎◎	726
	●●	725
	✕✕	471
	⊠⊠	BLANC
		939

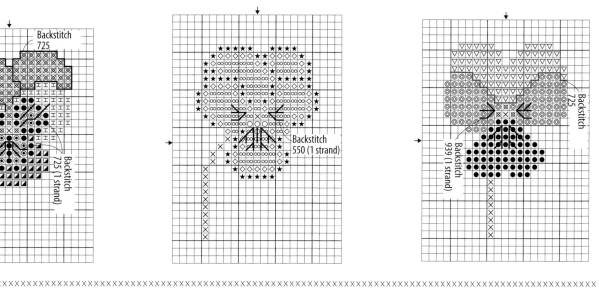

Backstitch
725

Backstitch
939 (1 strand)

Black Jack

●●	823
○○	725
**	792
××	471
∞∞	BLANC
	310

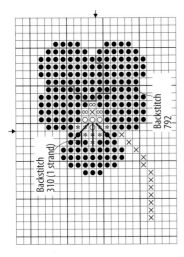

Backstitch 310 (1 strand)

Backstitch 792

Blue Face

▽▽	210
♠♠	553
○○	725
××	471
∞∞	BLANC
	823

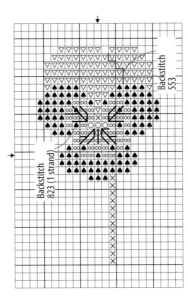

Backstitch 553

Backstitch 823 (1 strand)

Baby Light Blue (back view)

♡♡	340
◣◣	3746
××	471
HH	3347

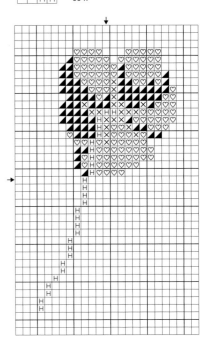

Velour Blue Bronze

△△	632
♥♥	333
◎◎	938
○○	725
××	471
∞∞	BLANC
	3371

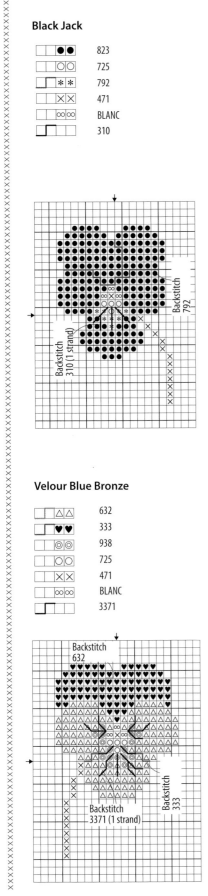

Backstitch 632

Backstitch 333

Backstitch 3371 (1 strand)

Blueberry Cream

♥♥	553
★★	554
××	746
◎◎	726
××	471
⊠⊠	BLANC
	823

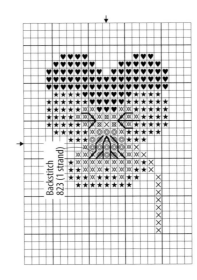

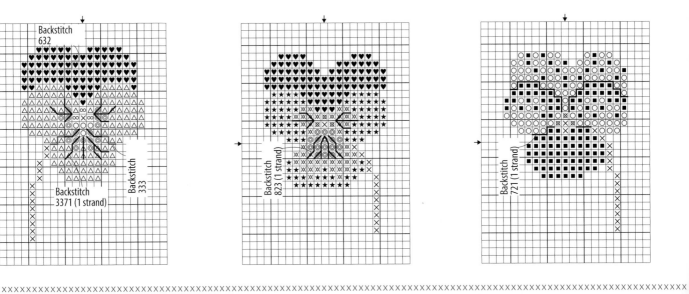

Backstitch 823 (1 strand)

Fancy Mix

○○	972
■■	741
××	471
⊠⊠	BLANC
	721

Backstitch 721 (1 strand)

Common Wildflowers

Shown on pages 14–15

Sampler

Materials:

» 40 x 40cm (15¾ x 15¾in) of DMC 11-count linen in 3865
» No. 25 embroidery floss (refer to chart for DMC colour numbers)

Finished Size:

» 21.5 x 22.5cm (8½ x 9in)

Motifs

Materials (for one motif):

» 20 x 30cm (8 x 11¾in) of DMC 11-count linen in 3865
» No. 25 embroidery floss (refer to charts for DMC colour numbers)
» Small white tag

Finished Size:

» A: 4.5 x 18cm (1¾ x 7in)
» B: 6 x 20cm (2½ x 8in)
» C: 4.5 x 18.5cm (1¾ x 7¼in)

Green

◆ ◆	3348
✕ ✕	3346
✦ ✦	3012
● ●	987
丄 丄	989

Red/Pink

♡ ♡	3608
☆ ☆	915
⊞ ⊞	309

Yellow/Orange

⊠ ⊠	3822
✿ ✿	783

Purple

⊘ ⊘	554
∞ ∞	553

Blue

▽ ▽	794
■ ■	931

Brown

▼ ▼	3045

Grey

⊙ ⊙	844

Cream

z z	822

Backstitch
844 (1 strand)

Backstitch
3348

Backstitch
989

Backstitch
931

Backstitch
844 (1 strand)

Backstitch
989

Backstitch
844

Backstitch
3348

Backstitch
989

Backstitch
309 (1 strand)

French knot
844

Backstitch
844 (1 strand)

Instructions

Stitch the flower motif. Write the plant name on the small white tag. Attach the tag to the stem by stitching the tag's thread to the fabric.

Yellow/Orange

⊚ ⊚	677
Z Z	726
⋈ ⋈	3822
◢ ◢	977

Red/Pink

⊠ ⊠	3688
▼ ▼	3350

Blue

♡ ♡	3325
◢◢	931

Green

× ×	368
✴ ✴	987
● ●	988
■ ■	989
☆ ☆	3348
♠ ♠	3012
◎ ◎	320

Shepherd's Purse

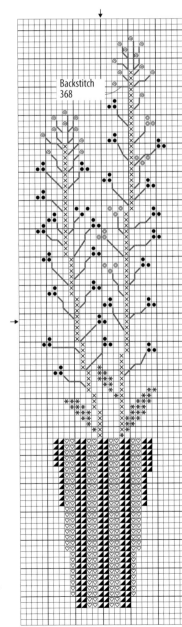

Backstitch 368

Common Vetch

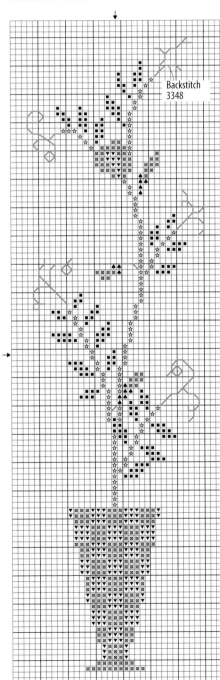

Backstitch 3348

Indian Strawberry

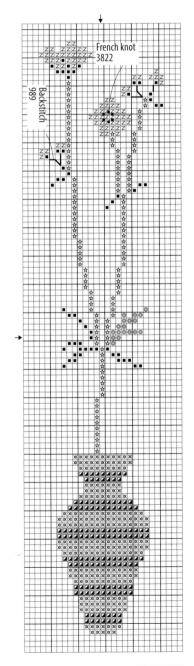

French knot 3822

Backstitch 989

Red Poppy Collage

Shown on page 16

Materials:

» Four scraps of neutral embroidery fabric (should measure 40 x 45cm [15¾ x 17¾in] when sewn together)
» 30 x 35cm (11¾ x 13¾in) of waste canvas
» 50 x 50cm (19¾ x 19¾in) of lightweight fusible interfacing
» No. 25 embroidery floss (refer to chart for DMC colour numbers)
» 25cm (9¾in) of red tape measure print ribbon

Finished Size:

» 22.5 x 28cm (9 x 11in)

Instructions

1. Sew the scraps of embroidery fabric together to create a patchwork background fabric measuring 40 x 45cm (15¾ x 17¾in). Adhere lightweight fusible interfacing to the wrong side of the embroidery fabric.

2. Appliqué the ribbon to the embroidery fabric following the placement indicated in the chart on page 69.

3. Baste the waste canvas to the embroidery fabric (refer to page 105 for instructions on using waste canvas). Stitch the poppy motif, then remove the waste canvas.

Close-up view of the poppy cross-stitch motif

Close-up view of the appliquéd ribbon detail

Green

	✕	✕	368
	♠	♠	989
	▽	▽	988
	◢	◢	367

Red

	○	○	3801
	☆	☆	321
	♥	♥	816

Brown

	◆	◆	869

Blue

	■	■	939

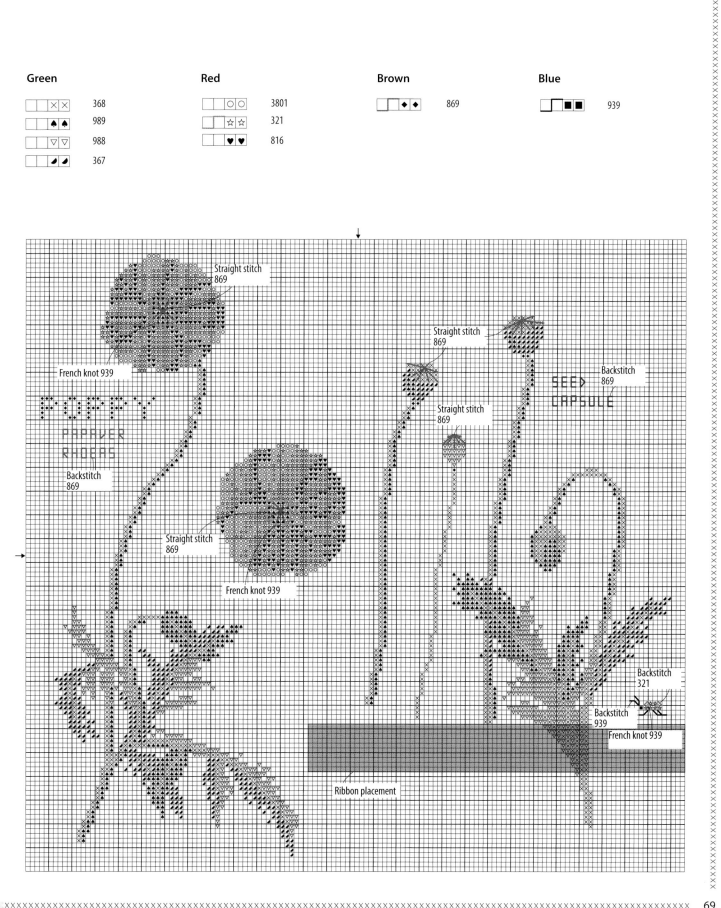

Straight stitch 869

Straight stitch 869

Backstitch 869

French knot 939

Straight stitch 869

SEED CAPSULE

PAPAVER RHOEAS

Backstitch 869

Straight stitch 869

French knot 939

Backstitch 321

Backstitch 939

French knot 939

Ribbon placement

Wildflower Garden Motifs

Shown on pages 19–21

Wild mignonette

Materials (for one motif):

» 30 x 35cm (11¾ x 13¾in) of DMC 11-count linen in 3865

» No. 25 embroidery floss (refer to charts for DMC colour numbers)

Finished Size:

» White clover: 10.5 x 16cm (4¼ x 6¼in)
» Meadow crane's bill: 11 x 17.5cm (4¼ x 7in)
» Red campion: 10.5 x 18cm (4¼ x 7in)
» Wild pansy: 10.5 x 18.5cm (4¼ x 7¼in)
» Everlasting pea: 10.5 x 20.5cm (4¼ x 8in)
» Wild mignonette: 12 x 21cm (4¾ x 8¼in)

Green		Brown		Cream	
✱✱	966	ⲓⲓ	407	‖‖	822
✕✕	989	●●	3045		
○○	367	◆◆	640		
◢◢	502				

Green		Brown		Purple	
✕✕	368	◆◆	640	♡♡	340
●●	987	⊠⊠	3722	✚✚	3746
▽▽	988	‖‖	3828	**Grey**	645
				(for French knots)	

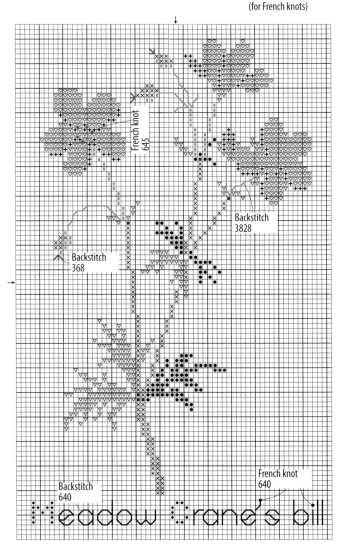

French knot 645

Backstitch 3828

Backstitch 368

Backstitch 640

French knot 640

Meadow crane's bill

French knot 640

Backstitch 640

White clover

70

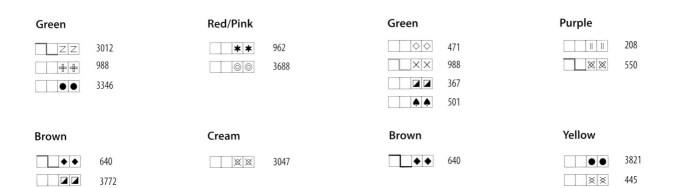

Green

	Z Z	3012
	✛ ✛	988
	● ●	3346

Red/Pink

	✳ ✳	962
	◎ ◎	3688

Green

	◇ ◇	471
	✕ ✕	988
	◧ ◧	367
	♠ ♠	501

Purple

	‖ ‖	208
	⊠ ⊠	550

Brown

	◆ ◆	640
	◨ ◨	3772

Cream

	⊠ ⊠	3047

Brown

	◆ ◆	640

Yellow

	● ●	3821
	⊠ ⊠	445

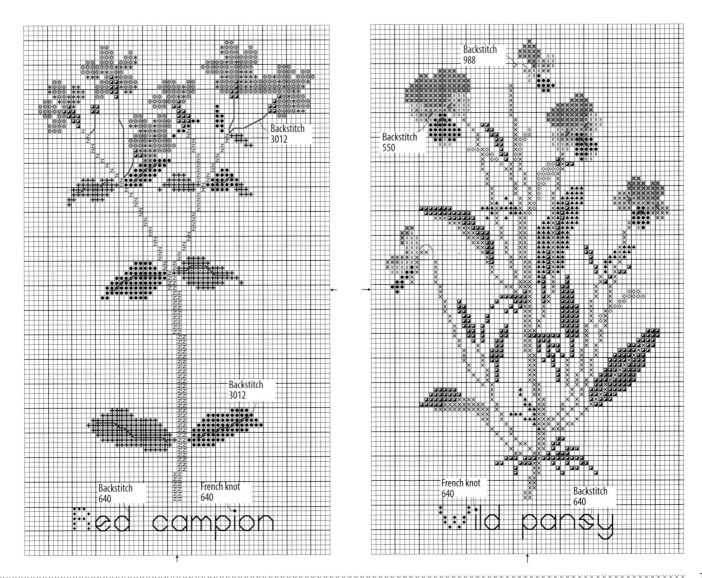

Backstitch 3012

Backstitch 3012

Backstitch 640

French knot 640

Red campion

Backstitch 988

Backstitch 550

French knot 640

Backstitch 640

Wild pansy

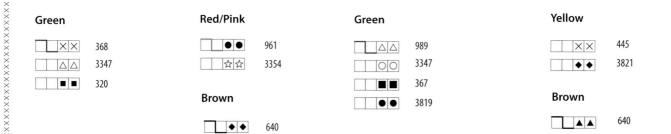

Green

	368
××	368
△△	3347
■■	320

Red/Pink

●●	961
☆☆	3354

Brown

◆◆	640

Green

△△	989
○○	3347
■■	367
●●	3819

Yellow

××	445
◆◆	3821

Brown

▲▲	640

Backstitch 961

Backstitch 368

Backstitch 989

French knot 640

Backstitch 640

French knot 640

Backstitch 640

everlasting pea

ild mignonette

Wildflower Garden Sampler

Shown on page 18

Materials:

» 50 x 60cm (19¾ x 23¾in) of DMC 11-count linen in 3865

» No. 25 embroidery floss (refer to chart for DMC colour numbers)

Finished Size:

» 27.5 x 45cm (10¾ x 17¾in)

Green

××	368
⊘⊘	989
⊹⊹	988
▲▲	320
♡♡	987
⋈⋈	3346
☆☆	471
◇◇	3012
●●	3815
✳✳	3819

Brown

★★	3828
⊕⊕	922
◪◪	3772

Pink

ZZ	3688
✳✳	3687
♥♥	962

Purple

◆◆	209
∞∞	327

Blue

⊗⊗	793
⊠⊠	340

Grey

♠♠	645
■■	647

Yellow/Orange

✤✤	445
⊙⊙	3821

Cream

⊃⊃	822

Note: The large cross-stitch chart spreads onto two pages. Two columns of stitches are repeated on each portion of the chart in order to indicate where the motif should overlap. Align the semicircles on each portion of the chart so they form complete circles. I recommend photocopying the charts and taping the sheets of paper together to create one large chart.

Align circles to combine chart. Refer to page 73 for details.

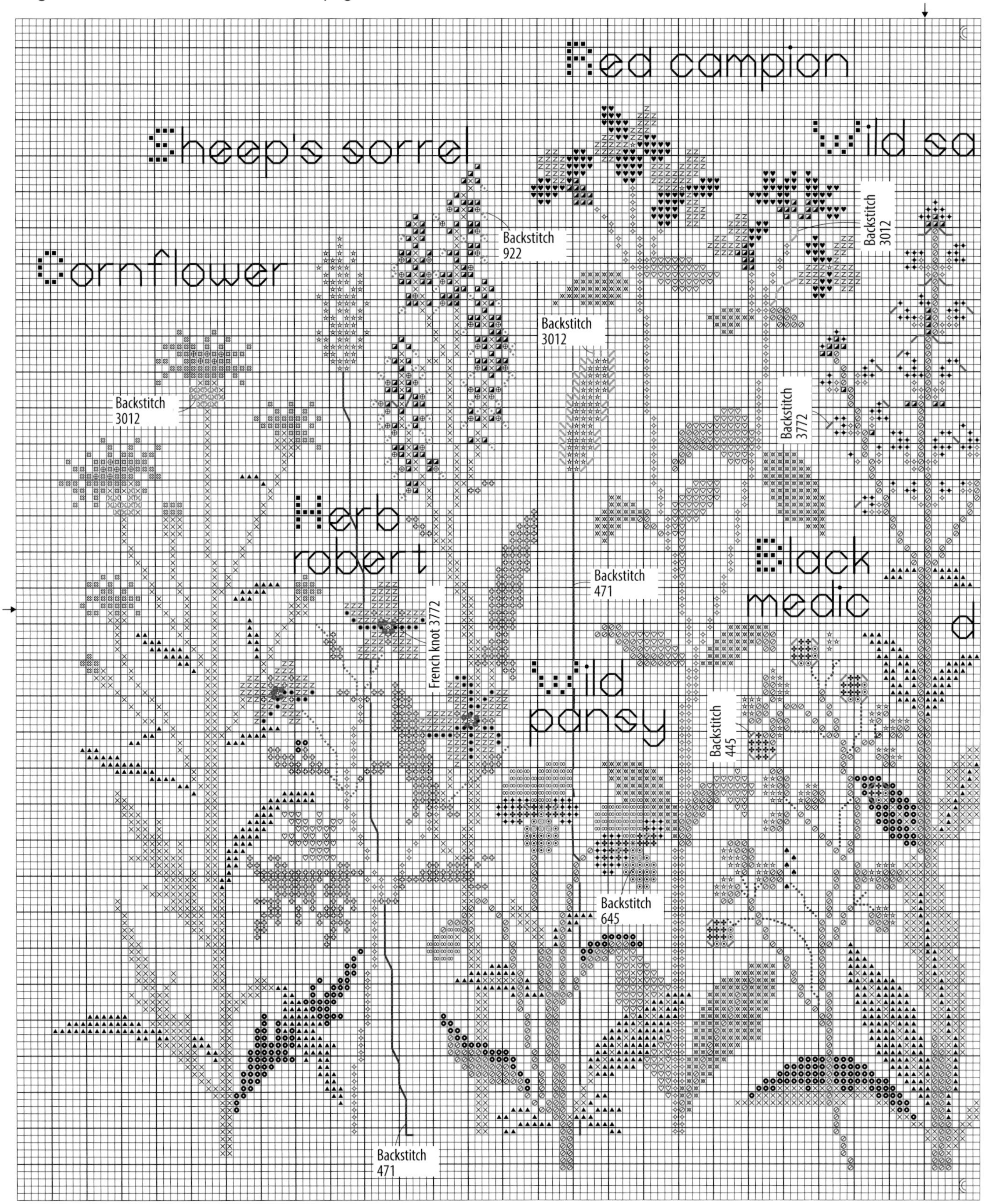

Red campion

Sheep's sorrel

Wild sa

Cornflower

Backstitch 922

Backstitch 3012

Backstitch 3012

Backstitch 3772

Backstitch 3012

Herb robert

Backstitch 471

Black medic

d

French knot 3772

Wild pansy

Backstitch 445

Backstitch 645

Backstitch 471

Cowparsley

age

Backstitch
368

Meadow
Crane's bill

Backstitch
988

Backstitch
647

Backstitch
471

French knot 647

Wild
migno-
nette

French knot 645

Backstitch
471

Backstitch
989

Henbit
dead-net

White clover

Backstitch
471

Wild Rose Sampler

Shown on page 22

Materials:

» 30 x 40cm (11¾ x 15¾in) of DMC
  11-count linen in 3865
» No. 25 embroidery floss (refer to chart
  for DMC colour numbers)

Finished Size:

» 23 x 24cm (9 x 9½in)

Green

⊞⊞	320
▲▲	3346
✕✕	989
●●	987
◎◎	367
◢◢	471

Red/Pink

♡♡	761
✕✕	3733
◆◆	3731
♥♥	309
✱✱	948
⊗⊗	3721

Brown

■■	3772
∞∞	371

Grey

	646

Off-White

‖‖	ECRU

Yellow 3821
(for French knots)

Backstitch
3346

French knot
3821

Backstitch
3772

Note: The large cross-stitch chart spreads onto two pages. Two columns of stitches are repeated on each portion of the chart in order to indicate where the motif should overlap. Align the semicircles on each portion of the chart so they form complete circles. I recommend photocopying the charts and taping the sheets of paper together to create one large chart.

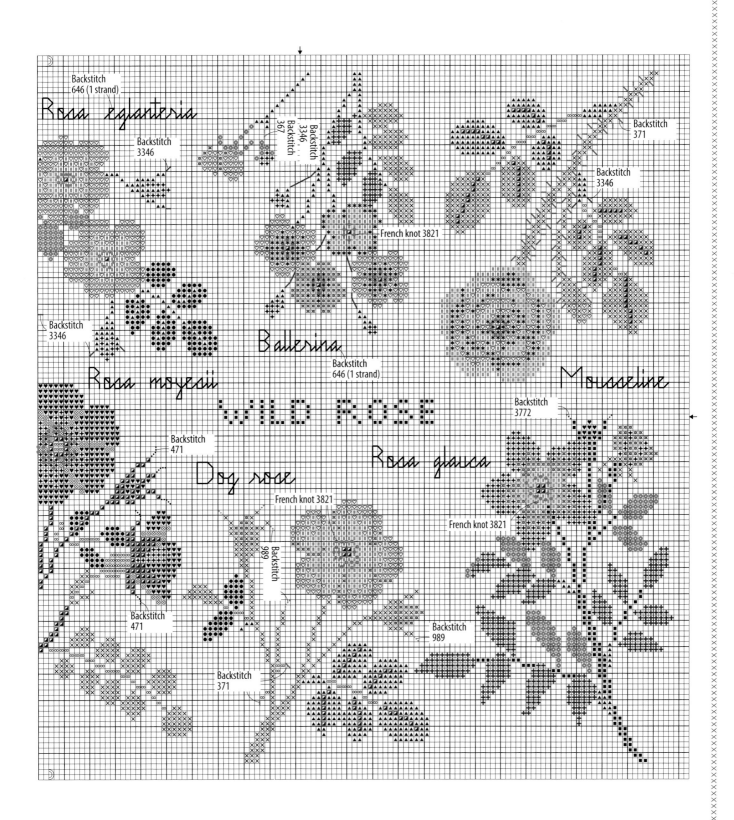

Wild Rose Journal

Shown on page 24

Materials:

» Outside cover: 25 x 30cm (9¾ x 11¾in) of khaki linen
» Inside cover: 20 x 25cm (8 x 9¾in) of DMC 11-count linen in 3865
» Interior pages: 20 x 70cm (8 x 27½in) of DMC 11-count linen in 3865
» 20 x 25cm (8 x 9¾in) of heavyweight fusible interfacing
» 20 x 25cm (8 x 9¾in) of medium-weight fusible interfacing
» No. 25 embroidery floss (refer to chart for DMC colour numbers)
» 25cm (9¾in) of 0.4cm (¼in) wide ribbon

Finished Size:

» Embroidery: 13.5 x 20cm (5¼ x 8in)
» Journal: 16.5 x 23.5cm (6½ x 9¼in)

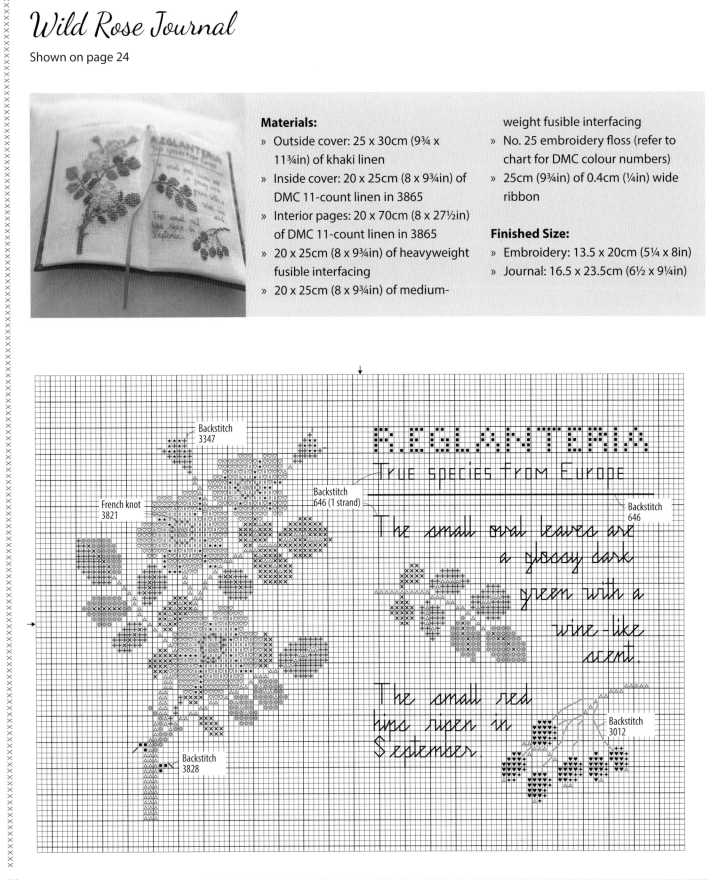

Green

⊘ ⊘	3819
△ △	3012
⊞ ⊞	3347
◎ ◎	989
✕ ✕	987

Red/Pink

♡ ♡	3354
★ ★	3733
♥ ♥	3328
✦ ✦	3721

Brown

■ ■	3828

Off-White

‖ ‖	ECRU

Grey

	646

Yellow
(for French knots)

3821

Heavyweight Fusible Interfacing

Medium-weight Fusible Interfacing, Inside Cover & Interior Pages

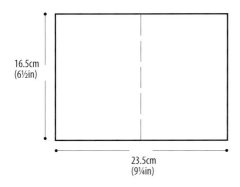

16.5cm (6½in)

23.5cm (9¼in)

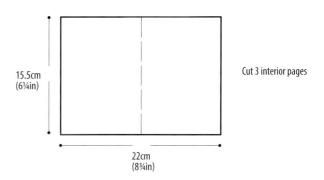

15.5cm (6¼in)

22cm (8¾in)

Cut 3 interior pages

Instructions

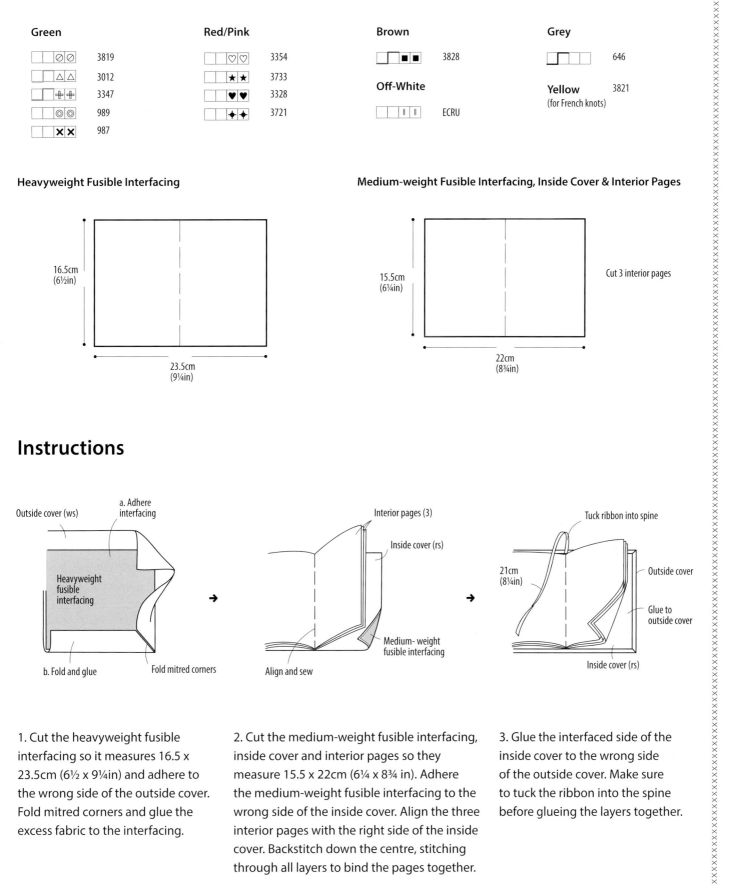

Outside cover (ws)

a. Adhere interfacing

Heavyweight fusible interfacing

b. Fold and glue

Fold mitred corners

Interior pages (3)

Inside cover (rs)

Medium-weight fusible interfacing

Align and sew

Tuck ribbon into spine

21cm (8¼in)

Outside cover

Glue to outside cover

Inside cover (rs)

1. Cut the heavyweight fusible interfacing so it measures 16.5 x 23.5cm (6½ x 9¼in) and adhere to the wrong side of the outside cover. Fold mitred corners and glue the excess fabric to the interfacing.

2. Cut the medium-weight fusible interfacing, inside cover and interior pages so they measure 15.5 x 22cm (6¼ x 8¾ in). Adhere the medium-weight fusible interfacing to the wrong side of the inside cover. Align the three interior pages with the right side of the inside cover. Backstitch down the centre, stitching through all layers to bind the pages together.

3. Glue the interfaced side of the inside cover to the wrong side of the outside cover. Make sure to tuck the ribbon into the spine before glueing the layers together.

Berry Motifs

Shown on page 26

Materials (for one motif):

» 25 x 25cm (9¾ x 9¾in) of 10-count linen in white
» No. 25 embroidery floss (refer to charts for DMC colour numbers)
» 2mm diameter round beads
  • Bramble motif: 50 red and 65 purple
  • Raspberry motif: 125 red
  • Blueberry motif: 100 blue

Finished Size:

» Bramble motif: 11.5 x 12cm (4½ x 4¾in)
» Raspberry motif: 10 x 12.5cm (4 x 5in)
» Blueberry motif: 11.5 x 12.5cm (4½ x 5in)

Note: Sew the beads on after completing the cross-stitch motif. There's no need to count the beads, just use the amount necessary to fill the outline of the berry.

Green

	⊙ ⊙	3345
	✕ ✕	987
	▽ ▽	989
	◨ ◨	3012
	✢ ✢	734

Pink

	♡ ♡	819

Brown

	■ ■	640

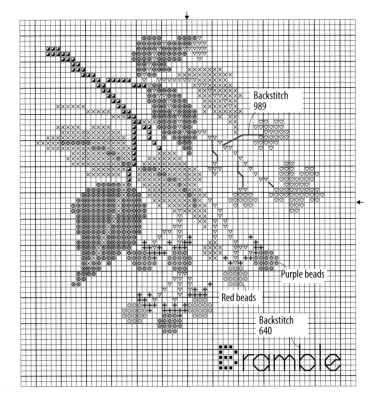

Backstitch 989

Purple beads

Red beads

Backstitch 640

Green

	= =	472
□ □	471
⊘ ⊘	988
▽ ▽	907
■ ■	470

Brown

| ⊙ ⊙ | 832 |
| ◆ ◆ | 640 |

Pink

| ♥ ♥ | 758 |

Green

■ ■	368
□ □	367
✕ ✕	320

Brown/Orange

⊕ ⊕	783
▽ ▽	436
◆ ◆	640

Blue

| ☆ ☆ | 3807 |

Grey

| ♠ ♠ | 844 |

Cream

| = = | 822 |

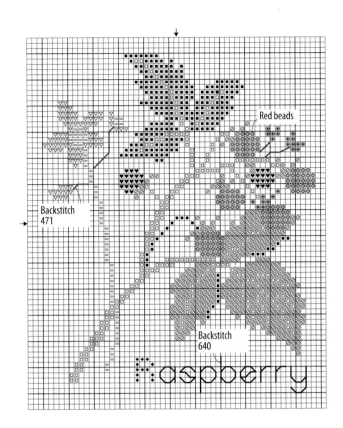

Red beads

Backstitch 471

Backstitch 640

raspberry

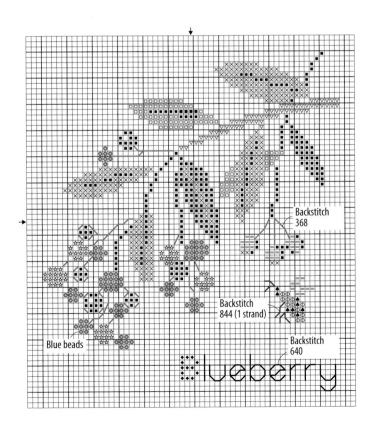

Backstitch 368

Backstitch 844 (1 strand)

Backstitch 640

Blue beads

blueberry

Berry Tote Bag

Shown on page 29

Materials:

- » Outside fabric: 30 x 80cm (11¾ x 31½in) of 10-count linen in natural
- » Lining fabric: 30 x 80cm (11¾ x 31½in) of satin
- » 30 x 80cm (11¾ x 31½in) of fusible interfacing
- » 10 x 55cm (4 x 21¾in) of Vilene fusible elastic interfacing
- » No. 25 embroidery floss (refer to chart for DMC colour numbers)
- » 2mm diameter round beads
  - • 225 red
  - • 115 purple
- » Two 1.4 x 40cm (⅝ x 15¾in) leather handles

Finished Size:

- » Embroidery: 18 x 22.5cm (7 x 9in)
- » Bag: 25 x 35cm (9¾ x 13¾in)

Instructions

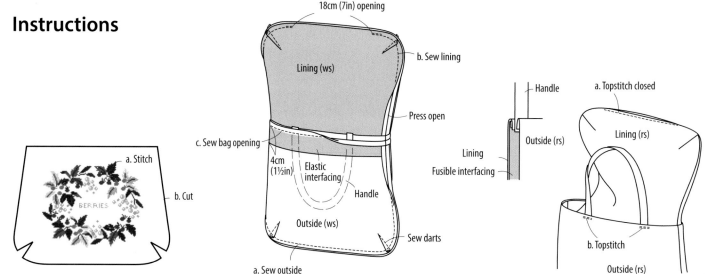

1. Stitch the motif onto the outside fabric. Note: Sew the beads on after completing the cross-stitch motif. There's no need to count the beads, just use the amount necessary to fill the outline of the berry. Cut the two outside pieces, two lining pieces and two fusible interfacing pieces into shape following the measurements in the diagram on page 83.

2. Sew the darts on each outside piece. Adhere the elastic interfacing to the wrong side of each outside piece along the bag opening. Align the two outside pieces with right sides together and sew. Press the seam allowance open. Adhere fusible interfacing to the wrong side of each lining piece and sew the darts. Align the two lining pieces with right sides together and sew, leaving an 18cm (7in) opening. With right sides together, insert the lining into the bag outside. Sandwich the handles in between the two layers following the placement noted in the diagram on page 83. Sew around the bag opening.

3. Turn the bag right side out through the opening. Press the seam allowances in and topstitch the lining opening closed. Topstitch the handles in place on the bag outside.

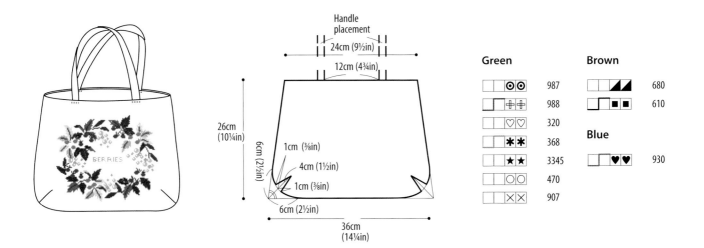

Green

	⊙	⊙	987
	⊞	⊞	988
	♡	♡	320
	✶	✶	368
	★	★	3345
	○	○	470
	✕	✕	907

Brown

	◢	◢	680
	■	■	610

Blue

	♥	♥	930

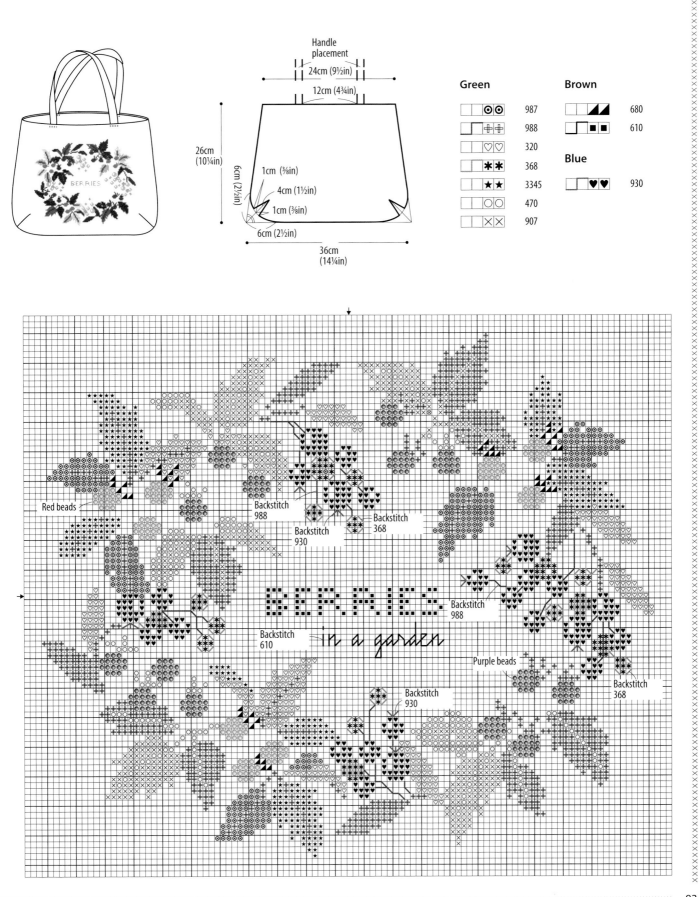

Red beads

Backstitch 988

Backstitch 930

Backstitch 368

Backstitch 988

Backstitch 610

in a garden

Purple beads

Backstitch 368

Backstitch 930

Christmas Rose Motifs

Shown on page 30

Materials:

White Christmas Rose

» 25 x 25cm (9¾ x 9¾in) of DMC 11-count linen in 842

» No. 25 embroidery floss (refer to chart for DMC colour numbers)

Pink Christmas Rose

» 40 x 45cm (15¾ x 17¾in) of DMC 11-count linen in 3865

» No. 25 embroidery floss (refer to chart for DMC colour numbers)

Finished Size:

» White Christmas Rose: 11 x 12.5cm (4¼ x 5in)

» Pink Christmas Rose: 24 x 28.5cm (9½ x 11¼in)

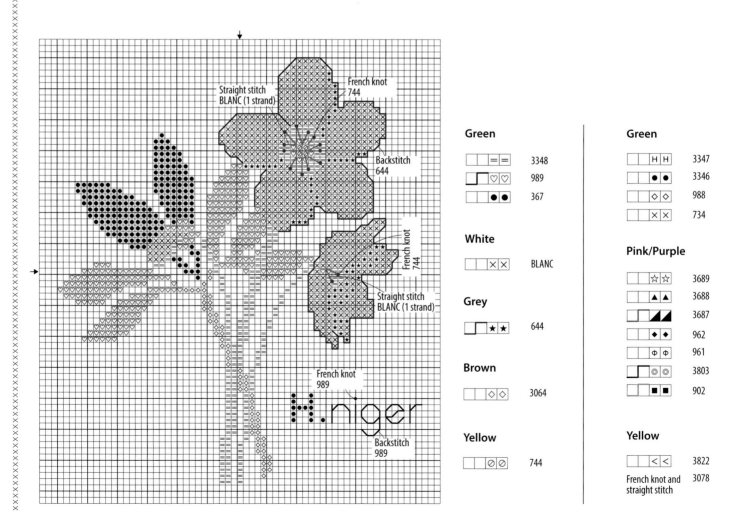

Straight stitch BLANC (1 strand)

French knot 744

Backstitch 644

French knot 744

Straight stitch BLANC (1 strand)

French knot 989

Backstitch 989

Green			
	=	=	3348
	♡	♡	989
	●	●	367

White			
	×	×	BLANC

Grey			
	★	★	644

Brown			
	◇	◇	3064

Yellow			
	⊘	⊘	744

Green			
	H	H	3347
	●	●	3346
	◇	◇	988
	×	×	734

Pink/Purple			
	☆	☆	3689
	▲	▲	3688
	◥	◢	3687
	◆	◆	962
	φ	φ	961
	◎	◎	3803
	■	■	902

Yellow			
	<	<	3822

French knot and straight stitch 3078

Close-Up Charts for Flower Centres

After completing the cross-stitch motif, embroider the centre of each flower using French knots and straight stitch (1 strand).

A

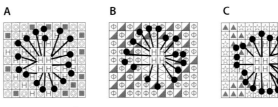

B

C

D

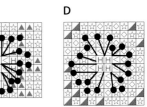

Backstitch
3687

Backstitch
3687

Backstitch
3803

French knot
3803

Orientalis
Hybrid

Backstitch
3803

Helleborus

Backstitch
3803

B

C

A

Backstitch
3687

Backstitch
902

D

Backstitch
3687

Yellow Flowers & Blue Flowers

Shown on pages 32 & 33

Materials (for one motif):

» 30 x 30cm (11¾ x 11¾in) of DMC 11-count linen in 3865
» No. 25 embroidery floss (refer to charts for DMC colour numbers)

Finished Size:

» 20 x 20cm (8 x 8in)

VIOLA

MIMOSA

Backstitch 368

TANGUTICA

TULIPA

Backstitch 726

Backstitch 844

RANUNCULUS

Backstitch 844

EURYOPS DAISY

Yellow Flower Motif

Green
⊘ ⊘	3348
∞ ∞	988
× ×	368
● ●	320

Yellow/Orange
○ ○	3078
♥ ♥	726
□ □	725
★ ★	783

Beige
■ ■	3828

Blue
◆ ◆	932

Grey
◎ ◎	844

Blue Flower Motif

Green
Z Z	3348
∞ ∞	471
× ×	988
♠ ♠	367

Yellow/Orange
◎ ◎	775
■ ■	3807
○ ○	3746
★ ★	791
▽ ▽	792
⊘ ⊘	794

Beige
◆ ◆	642

Grey
* *	844

Yellow
♥ ♥	3821

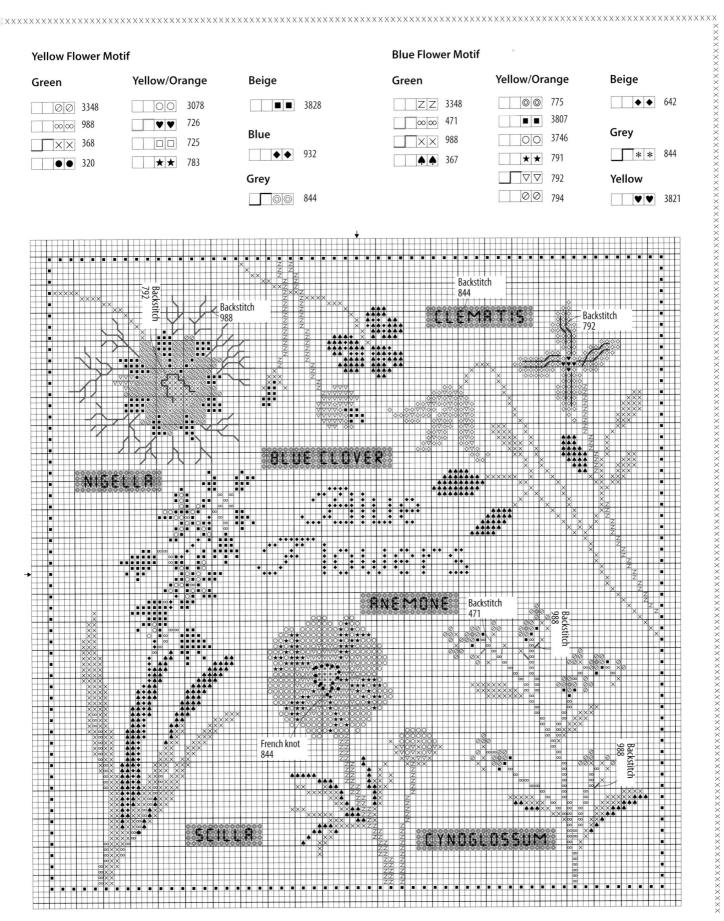

Swedish Wildflowers Collage

Shown on page 34

Materials:

» Embroidery fabric:
- A & B: 10 x 15cm (4 x 6in) of DMC 11-count linen in 3865
- C: 25 x 25cm (9¾ x 9¾in) of DMC 11-count linen in 3742
- D: 8 x 8cm (3⅛ x 3⅛in) of DMC 11-count linen in 842
- E: 15 x 15cm (6 x 6in) of DMC 11-count linen in 842
- F & G: 8 x 25cm (3⅛ x 9¾in) of DMC 11-count linen in 3865
- H: 8 x 10cm (3⅛ x 8in) of DMC 11-count linen in 3865

» Base fabric: Scraps of white fabric

(should measure 40 x 50cm [15¾ x 19¾in] when sewn together)

» No. 25 embroidery floss (refer to charts for DMC colour numbers)

Finished Size:

» A: 4.5 x 6.5cm (1¾ x 2½in)
» B: 4.5 x 9.5cm (1¾ x 3¾in)
» C: 12.5 x 15cm (5 x 6in)
» D: 3.5 x 4.5cm (1½ x 1¾in)
» E: 7 x 8cm (2¾ x 3⅛in)
» F: 2.5 x 19cm (1 x 7½in)
» G: 2.5 x 13.5cm (1 x 5¼in)
» H: 4 x 5cm (1½ x 2in)

Green

◎◎	3347
●●	3346
∞∞	3052
⊘⊘	3364
♠♠	988
□□	987
✕✕	704
●●	501
✳✳	471
❉❉	367

Yellow

◪◪	3047
⤬⤬	726
For French knots	744

Red/Pink

⊙⊙	3688
◆◆	3687
♣♣	3712
⊗⊗	3350
◇◇	309

Blue

✱✱	340
♥♥	792
✩✩	322
✳✳	930

Beige/Brown

◆◆	611
z z	610
⚘⚘	356
	640

Grey

♡♡	645

White

‖ ‖	BLANC
✛✛	ECRU

A

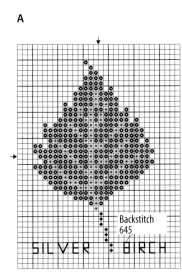

Backstitch
645

SILVER + BIRCH

B

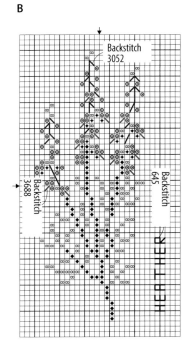

Backstitch
3052

Backstitch
3688

Backstitch
645

HEATHER

C

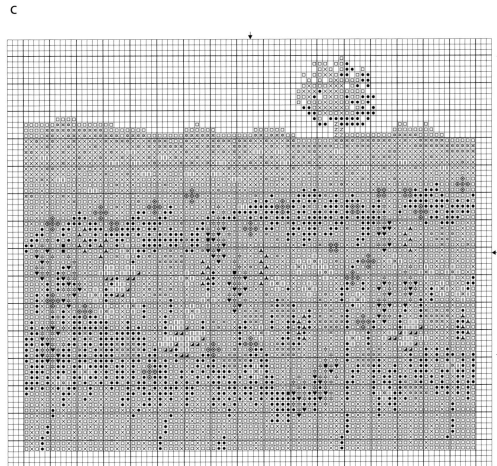

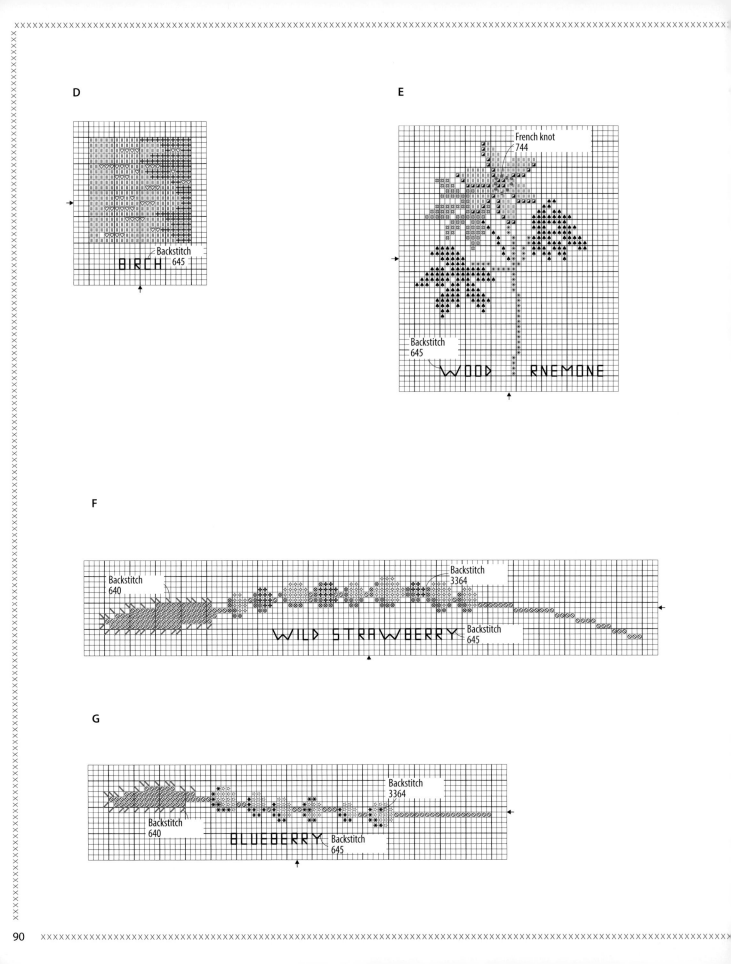

D

BIRCH

Backstitch
645

E

French knot
744

Backstitch
645

WOOD ANEMONE

F

Backstitch
640

Backstitch
3364

WILD STRAWBERRY

Backstitch
645

G

Backstitch
3364

Backstitch
640

BLUEBERRY

Backstitch
645

H

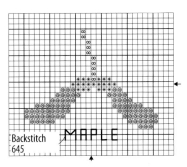

Layout Diagram

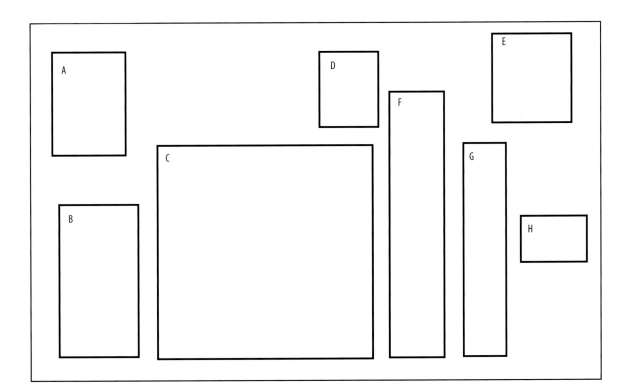

Position the completed cross-stitch motifs on the patchwork base fabric following the above diagram.

Swedish Wildflowers Sampler

Shown on page 35

Materials:

» 30 x 30cm (13¾ x 13¾in) of DMC
  11-count linen in 3782
» No. 25 embroidery floss (refer to chart
  for DMC colour numbers)

Finished Size:

» 19 x 21cm (7½ x 8¼in)

Green

✕✕	471
▽▽	368
✛✛	988
●●	987
ᴢᴢ	3348

Blue/Purple

⊙⊙	3807
✳✳	340
◑◑	208

Red/Pink

♥♥	3688
♣♣	350
✕✕	304

Yellow/Orange

◪◪	783
✳✳	743
■■	3047

White

‖‖	BLANC

Grey

✴✴	3799

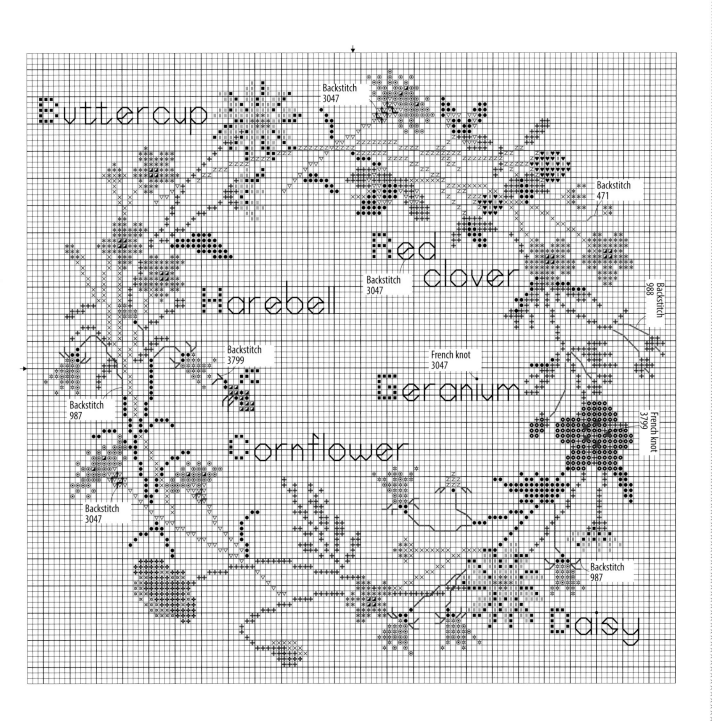

Wildlife Garden Collage

Shown on page 36

Materials:

» 45 x 50cm (17¾ x 19¾in) of DMC 11-count linen in 842 (for main flower motif)

» 10 x 10cm (4 x 4in) of DMC 11-count linen in 3865 (for frog motif)

» 15 x 20cm (6 x 8in) of DMC 11-count linen in 3865 (for seed bag motif)

» No. 25 embroidery floss

(refer to chart for DMC colour numbers)

» Small white tag

» Glue

Finished Size:

» Main flower motif: 20 x 32cm (8 x 12¾in)

» Frog motif: 5 x 6.5cm (2 x 2½in)

» Seed bag motif: 9 x 12.5cm (3½ x 5in)

Instructions

1. Stitch the main flower motif. Write "For ladybug" on the small white tag. Attach the tag to the stem of the pink flower by stitching the tag's thread to the fabric.

2. Stitch the frog motif. Trim the fabric to 5 x 6.5cm (2 x 2½in). Note: Do not add seam allowance—the raw edges are designed to be exposed. Glue the frog motif to the main flower motif, following the placement indicated on the cross-stitch chart on page 95.

3. Stitch the seed bag motif. Trim the fabric to 14 x 17.5cm (5½ x 7in). Note: These measurements include seam allowance. Fold the fabric over 2.5cm (1in) on each side and hemstitch the two sides and the bottom to the main flower motif to create a pocket.

Note: The large cross-stitch chart spreads onto two pages. Two columns of stitches are repeated on each portion of the chart in order to indicate where the motif should overlap. Align the semicircles on each portion of the chart so they form complete circles. I recommend photocopying the charts and taping the sheets of paper together to create one large chart.

Green

	××	368
	♡♡	987
	★★	988
	◆◆	3345
	○○	3012

Yellow/Orange

	△△	3821
	●●	783
	⊥⊥	3046

Red/Pink

	✢✢	3727
	◪◪	3726
	☆☆	347

White/Cream

	∞∞	BLANC
	◎◎	822

Black/Gray

	✦✦	310
	■■	844

Blue

	♠♠	794

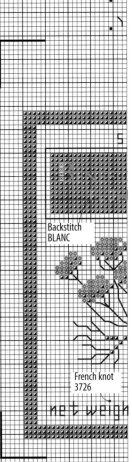

Backstitch
BLANC

French knot
3726

net weigh

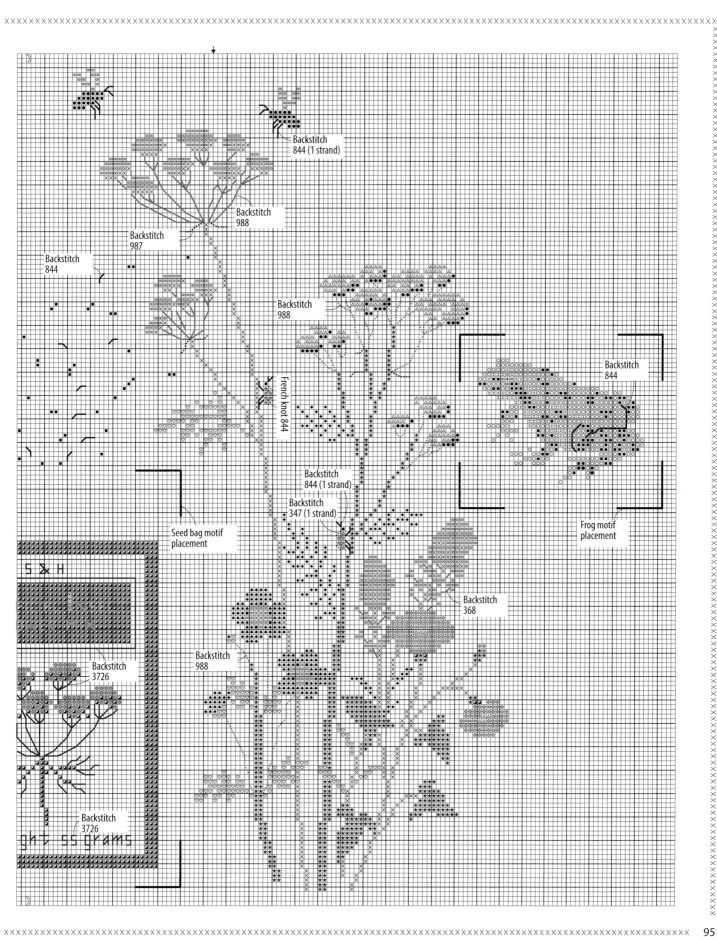

Backstitch
844 (1 strand)

Backstitch
988

Backstitch
987

Backstitch
844

Backstitch
988

Backstitch
844

French knot 844

Backstitch
844 (1 strand)

Backstitch
347 (1 strand)

Backstitch
844 (1 strand)

Backstitch
368

Seed bag motif
placement

Frog motif
placement

S & H

Backstitch
3726

Backstitch
988

Backstitch
3726

ght 55 grams

Gardening Pin Cushions

Shown on page 38

Materials (for one pin cushion):

» 12 x 12cm (4¾ x 4¾in) of DMC 11-count linen in 842
» No. 25 embroidery floss (refer to chart for DMC colour numbers)
» One ladybug or bee charm
» Polyester stuffing
» Cardboard scrap
» 5cm (2in) diameter metal lid

Finished Size:

» Embroidery: 3.5 x 6.5cm (1½ x 2½in) for A and 3.5 x 4.5cm (1½ x 1¾in) for B
» Pin Cushion: 6cm (2½in) diameter for A and 5cm (2in) diameter for B

Note: This project uses a 5cm (2in) diameter lid. You may need to adjust the size of your fabric if using a larger lid.

A

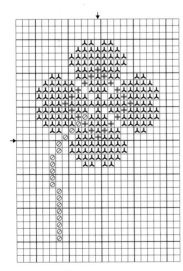

B

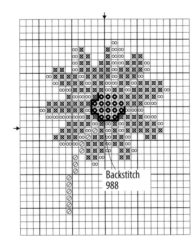

Backstitch
988

	人人	319
	⊕⊕	320
	⊘⊘	988
	●●	3820
	∞∞	3047
	⊠⊠	BLANC

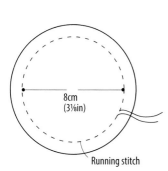

Running stitch

8cm
(3⅛in)

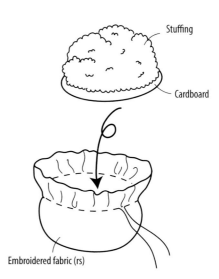

Stuffing

Cardboard

Embroidered fabric (rs)

1. Stitch the desired motif following the chart on page 96. Trim the embroidered fabric into a 10cm (4in) diameter circle (this measurement includes 1cm [⅜in] seam allowance). Running stitch along the seam allowance. Leave long thread tails.

2. Pull the thread tails to gather the embroidered fabric. Cut out a 5cm (2in) diameter cardboard circle. Glue the polyester stuffing to the cardboard. Insert the cardboard into the embroidered fabric and pull the thread tails taut.

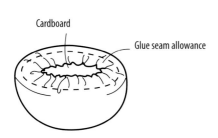

Cardboard

Glue seam allowance

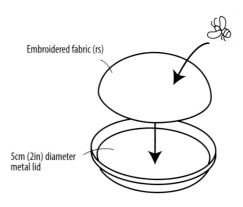

Embroidered fabric (rs)

5cm (2in) diameter
metal lid

3. Glue the seam allowance to the cardboard on the wrong side of the pin cushion.

4. Glue the pin cushion to the metal lid. Sew the charm to the pin cushion.

Gardening Sampler

Shown on page 39

Materials:

» 45 x 55cm (17¾ x 21¾in) of DMC 11-count linen in 3865
» No. 25 embroidery floss (refer to chart for DMC colour numbers)
» Shovel, watering can and scissors charms

Finished Size:

» 29 x 36.5cm (11½ x 14½in)

Note: Sew the charms on after completing the cross-stitch motif.

Green

♥	♥	368
◆	◆	471
✕	✕	988
●	●	320
✛	✛	367
✳	✳	501

Brown/Orange

⊠	⊠	3045
⊗	⊗	739
♡	♡	437
⋈	⋈	435
★	★	869
✳	✳	783

Blue

∞	∞	3755
⊙	⊙	334
■	■	931
▽	▽	3807

Purple

★	★	3746
☆	☆	554
Z	Z	208
❖	❖	327

Grey

✳	✳	3787
○	○	3024

Cream

◖	◗	822

Red

◉	◉	3328

Black

		310

Greenery Pillows

Shown on page 40

Materials (for one pillow):

» 45 x 90cm (17¾ x 35½in) of DMC 11-count linen in 842
» No. 25 embroidery floss (refer to charts for DMC colour numbers)
» One 35cm (14in) long zipper
» One 35 x 35cm (14 x 14in) pillow form

Finished Size:

» Embroidery: 23 x 23.5cm (9 x 9¼in) for A, 12 x 21cm (4¾ x 8¼in) for B and 6.5 x 25cm (2½ x 9¾in) for C
» Pillow: 36 x 36cm (14¼ x 14¼in)

A

	◪	◪	368
	+	+	3012
	◆	◆	3347
	○	○	987

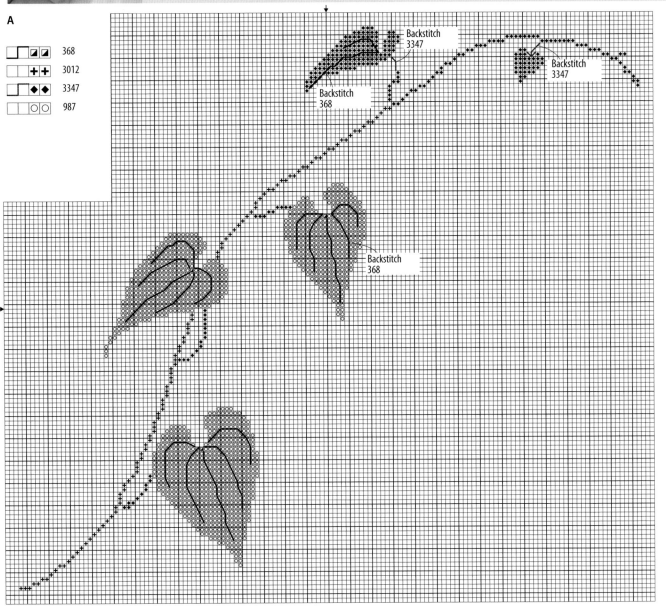

Backstitch 3347

Backstitch 368

Backstitch 3347

Backstitch 368

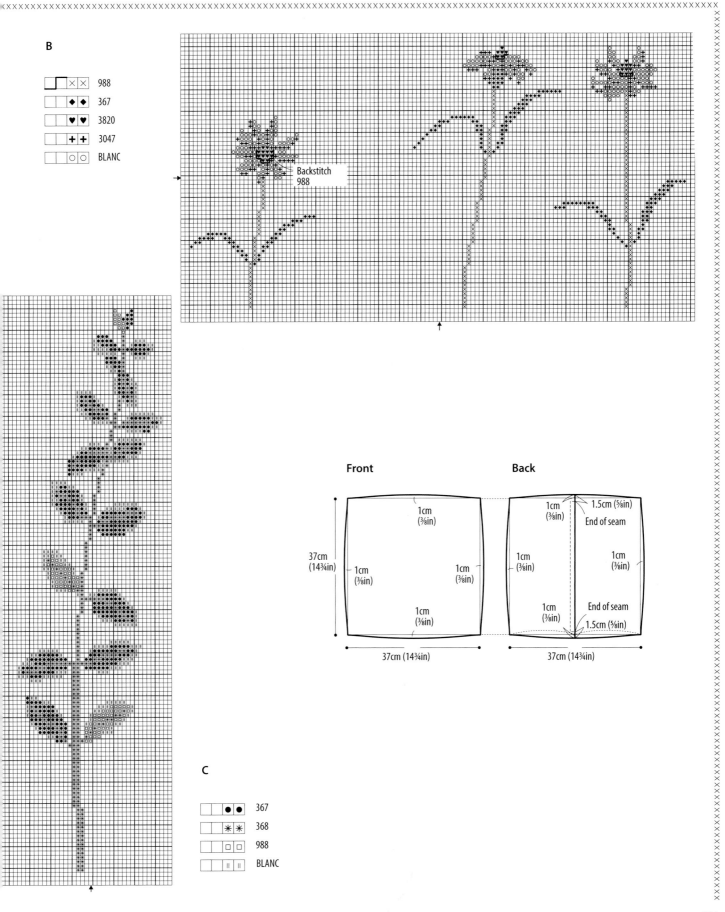

B

		988
×	×	
♦	♦	367
♥	♥	3820
+	+	3047
○	○	BLANC

Backstitch
988

Front

1cm (⅜in)

37cm (14¾in)

1cm (⅜in)

1cm (⅜in)

1cm (⅜in)

37cm (14¾in)

Back

1cm (⅜in)

1.5cm (⅝in)
End of seam

1cm (⅜in)

1cm (⅜in)

1cm (⅜in)

End of seam

1.5cm (⅝in)

37cm (14¾in)

C

		367
●	●	
✳	✳	368
□	□	988
‖	‖	BLANC

Instructions

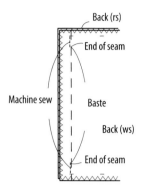

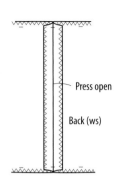

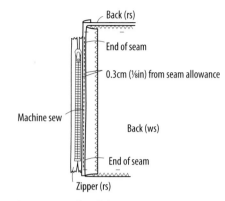

1. Cut a pillow front and two pillow backs following dimensions noted in the diagram on page 101. Stitch the desired motif onto the pillow front. Align the two back pieces with right sides together. Machine sew for 1.5cm (⅝in) starting at the seam allowance on both the top and bottom. Baste the two pieces together between the machine stitches.

2. Press the seam allowance open.

3. Sew one side of the zipper to each back piece, stitching about 0.3cm (⅛in) away from the seam allowance.

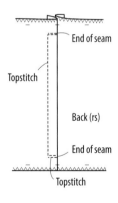

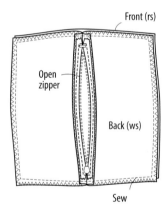

4. Topstitch around the zipper on the right side of the pillow back.

5. Open the zipper. Align the front and back with right sides together and sew around all four sides. Turn the pillow right side out through the open zipper.

Leaf Coasters

Shown on page 42

Materials (for one coaster):

» 15 x 30cm (6 x 11¾in) of DMC 11-count linen in 842
» No. 25 embroidery floss (refer to chart for DMC colour numbers)
» 28 small round beads in off-white
» Cardboard scrap

Finished Size:

» Embroidery: 3 x 3.5cm (1¼ x 1½in) for A, 3 x 3cm (1¼ x 1¼in) for B and 2.5 x 3cm (1 x 1¼in) for C
» Coaster: 10 x 10cm (4 x 4in)

A

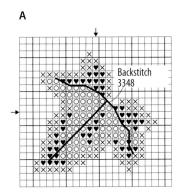

Backstitch 3348

B

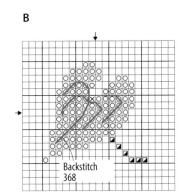

Backstitch 368

C

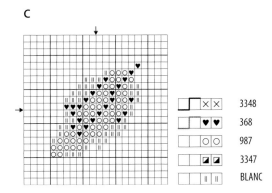

☐☐	✕✕	3348
☐☐	♥♥	368
☐☐	○○	987
☐☐	◢◢	3347
☐☐	‖ ‖	BLANC

Instructions

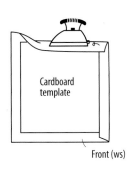

Cardboard template

Front (ws)

➡

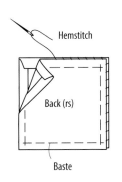

Hemstitch

Back (rs)

Baste

➡

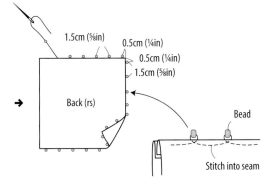

1.5cm (⅝in)
0.5cm (¼in)
0.5cm (¼in)
1.5cm (⅝in)

Back (rs)

Bead

Stitch into seam

1. Cut the linen in half to create two 15 x 15cm (6 x 6in) pieces. Stitch the desired motif onto the linen fabric to create the coaster front. Make a 10 x 10cm (4 x 4in) cardboard template. Use the template to fold and press the seam allowance of the embroidered fabric to the wrong side. Follow the same process to fold and press the seam allowance for the coaster back.

2. Align the front and back with right facing out and baste. Hemstitch the front and back together. Remove the basting stitches.

3. Backstitch the beads to the edge of the coaster, positioning the beads as shown in the above diagram. Stitch into coaster seam when attaching the beads.

Bee Apron

Shown on page 43

Materials:

» 15 x 25cm (6 x 9¾in) of waste canvas
» No. 25 embroidery floss (refer to
   chart for DMC colour numbers)
» One linen apron

Finished Size:

» 2.5 x 3cm (1 x 1¼in)

Instructions

1. Baste the waste canvas to the apron at the desired embroidery location.

2. Stitch the motifs through both the waste canvas and the apron.
Note: Make sure to position motif B on the diagonal.

3. Remove the basted stitches. Remove the waste canvas by unraveling the strands of the canvas.

A

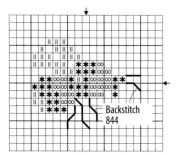

Backstitch
844

B

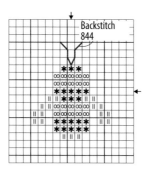

Backstitch
844

C

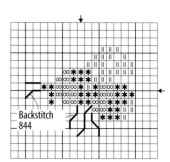

Backstitch
844

	|oo|oo|	783
	|✱|✱|	844
	|ll|ll|	ECRU

Embellished Dish Towels

Shown on page 44

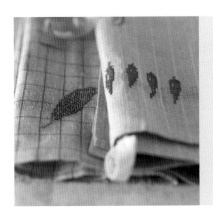

Materials (for one towel):

» One piece of waste canvas
  • A: 15 x 15cm (6 x 6in)
  • B: 15 x 20 cm (6 x 8in)
» No. 25 embroidery floss (refer to charts for DMC colour numbers)
» One linen dish towel

Finished Size:

» A: 4.5 x 6cm (1¾ x 2½in)
» B: 4.5 x 9.5cm (1¾ x 3¾in)

Instructions

1. Baste the waste canvas to the towel at the desired embroidery location.

2. Stitch the motif through both the waste canvas and the towel.

3. Remove the basted stitches. Remove the waste canvas by unraveling the strands of the canvas.

A

	□ □	370
	● ●	367
	× ×	434

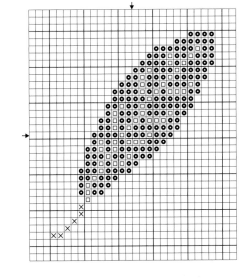

B

	● ●	367
	▲ ▲	498
	○ ○	347

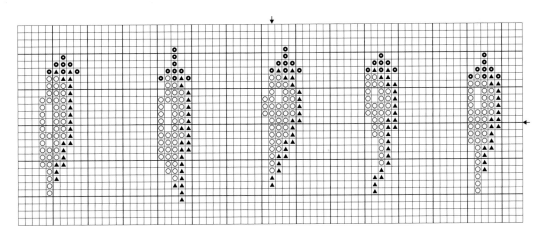

Seedlings Motif

Shown on page 46

Note: This project contains a few stitches that are formed over one vertical and one horizontal thread of the fabric. These stitches are marked by symbols that overlap multiple grid boxes in the chart below.

Materials:

» 30 x 35cm (11¾ x 13¾in) of DMC 11-count linen in 3865
» No. 25 embroidery floss (refer to chart for DMC colour numbers)

Finished Size:

» 13.5 x 17cm (5¼ x 6¾in)

 703

3348

320

987

989

For French knots 645

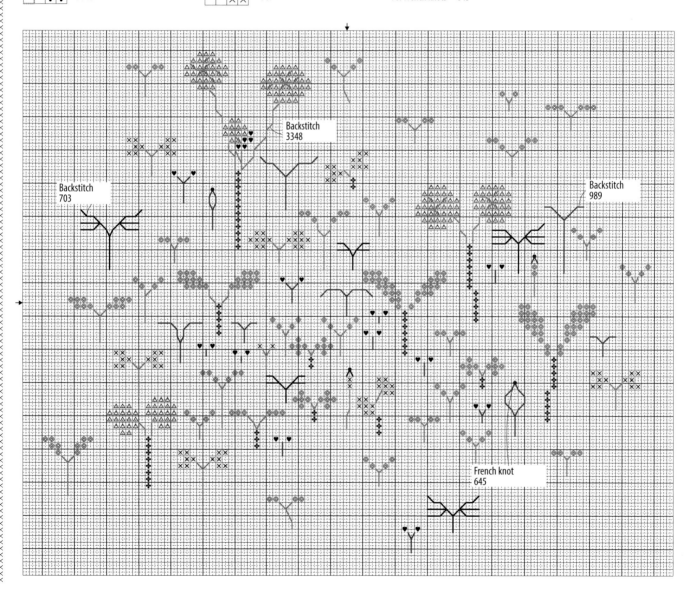

Backstitch 3348

Backstitch 703

Backstitch 989

French knot 645

Spring Bulbs

Shown on page 48

Materials:

» 40 x 50cm (15¾ x 19¾in) of DMC 11-count linen in 3866
» No. 25 embroidery floss (refer to chart for DMC colour numbers)
» 5 small white tags

Finished Size:

» 26.5 x 32.5cm (10 x 12¾in)

Instructions

Stitch the motif. If desired, write the plant names on the small white tags. Attach the tags to the stems by stitching the tag's thread to the fabric.

Close-up view of a tag on the Spring Bulbs sampler

Close-up view of the Spring Bulbs sampler

Green

☐	×	×	3348
☐	■	■	988
☐	✛	✛	320
☐	●	●	368
☐	⚶	⚶	367

Yellow/Orange

☐	✵	✵	745
☐	◇	◇	727
☐	⊠	⊠	725
☐	∞	∞	783

Brown

☐	✳	✳	422
☐	△	△	420
☐	◤	◤	610

Blue/Purple

☐	○	○	932
☐	⊙	⊙	3807
☐	◪	◪	3746

Pink

☐	♥	♥	3354

White

☐	‖	‖	BLANC

Grey

☐	◉	◉	844

Note: The large cross-stitch chart spreads onto two pages. Two columns of stitches are repeated on each portion of the chart in order to indicate where the motif should overlap. Align the semicircles on each portion of the chart so they form complete circles. I recommend photocopying the charts and taping the sheets of paper together to create one large chart.

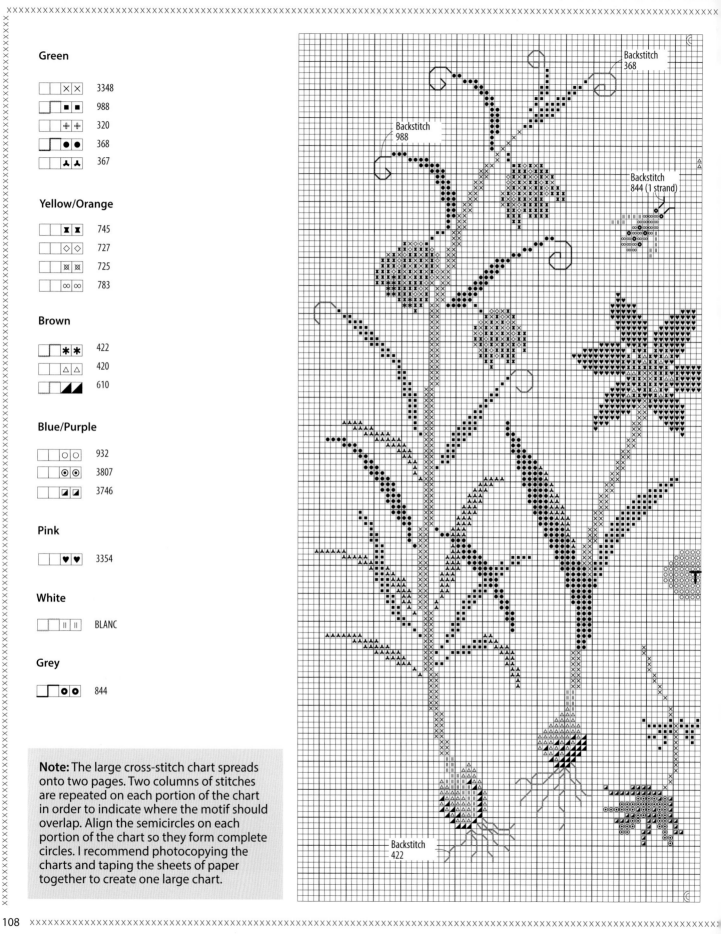

Backstitch 368

Backstitch 988

Backstitch 844 (1 strand)

Backstitch 422

French knot
988

Backstitch
988

Backstitch
610

Backstitch
BLANC

Backstitch
368

MUSCARI

Backstitch
844

TULIPA

Backstitch
988

Backstitch
422

Backstitch
422

Resources

UK

DMC
www.dmccreative.co.uk
Manufacturer of DMC cotton embroidery floss and fabric

Hobby Craft
www.hobbycraft.co.uk
National craft chain that carries DMC cotton embroidery floss, cross-stitch fabric and other stitching notions

Sew and So
www.sewandso.co.uk
Huge assortment of needlecraft tools, fabric and thread

Willow Fabrics
www.willowfabrics.com
Offers a variety of even weave fabrics, Vilene interfacing and beautiful threads

USA

123Stitch
www.123stitch.com
Excellent selection of cross-stitch fabric and threads

DMC
www.dmc-usa.com
Manufacturer of DMC cotton embroidery floss and fabric

Herrschners
www.herrschners.com
Great variety of needlework fabric, threads and frames

Jo-Ann Fabric and Craft Stores
www.joann.com
National craft chain that carries DMC cotton embroidery floss, fabric and other cross-stitch supplies